TEA SHOP WALKS
IN
LANCASHIRE

Clive Price

Published by Sigma Leisure – an imprint of
Sigma Press, 1 South Oak Lane, Wilmslow, Cheshire SK9 6AR, England.

British Library Cataloguing in Publication Data
A CIP record for this book is available from the British Library.

ISBN: 1-85058-582-2

Typesetting and Design by: Sigma Press, Wilmslow, Cheshire.

Cover: Rivington Pike from Lever Park *(Country Matters Picture Library; Copyright, Terry Marsh)*

Maps: Jeremy Semmens

Photographs: the author

Printed by: MFP Design & Print

Reprinted 1999

Disclaimer: the information in this book is given in good faith and is believed to be correct at the time of publication. No responsibility is accepted by either the author or publisher for errors or omissions, or for any loss or injury howsoever caused. Only you can judge your own fitness, competence and experience.

Acknowledgements

No book of this kind is a solo effort. In this particular instance, I have been very dependent on the co-operation of several other people.

In the first instance I owe a considerable debt of gratitude to Ron Sands of Lancaster City Tourism for his active encouragement, suggestions and hospitality. His staff in the Tourist Information Centre have also been generous in giving of their time and energy in dealing with my innumerable queries.

I must also thank the staffs of the various other Tourist Information Centres throughout Lancashire and, in particular, Mary Parker in Clitheroe for placing her local knowledge at my disposal.

As usual, the actual preparation of the book for publication was handled by Graham Beech and the staff of Sigma Press of Wilmslow and the finished product is testimony to their care and professionalism.

A book of this kind would not have been possible without the co-operation of the café owners who have shown that there is a real, genuine welcome to be found throughout Lancashire.

I am also grateful for the forbearance of my family during my absences from home and, in particular, I must mention my granddaughter, Tamsin. Whenever school holidays permitted, she accompanied me on many of the walks, so providing most welcome company and many observations which might otherwise have gone unnoticed.

Clive Price

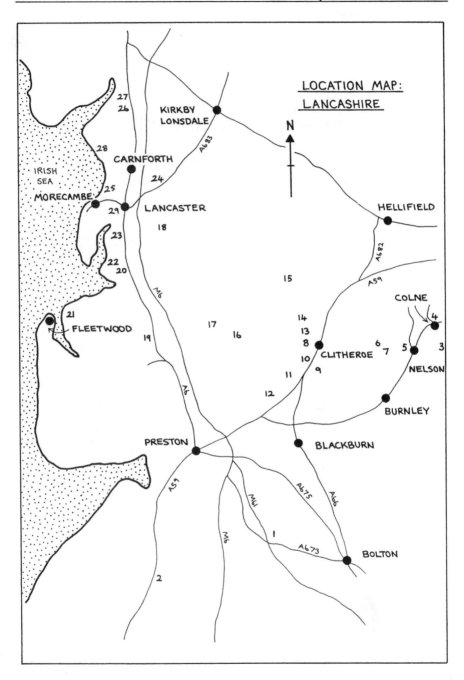

Contents

Introduction

The Walks

Lancashire

In many people's imagination, Lancashire is still a county of cloth caps, smoke-belching mills and factories, cobbled streets and terraced housing. However, in reality, the economic changes of recent years have removed many of these eyesores from the scene, although terraced housing still remains a feature of some towns. Factories and their drab surroundings have often disappeared to be replaced by attractive landscaping.

Sadly, for many walkers Lancashire is merely a county of passage as they hurtle along the M6 Motorway towards their desired mecca of the Lake District. They catch nothing more than momentary glimpses of the major scenic attractions on offer such as the West Pennine Moors, the Forest of Bowland and the great sweep of Morecambe Bay. They miss the detail of the landscape which transforms the county into a walker's paradise.

Originally Lancashire stretched from the River Mersey in the south to the boundary of Westmorland in the north and, beyond Morecambe Bay, included the ancient district of Furness. However, local government reorganisation of recent years has deprived the county of Furness along with the cities of Manchester, Liverpool, Salford and the major towns of Bolton, Bury, Rochdale, Oldham, Wigan and Warrington.

This truncated Lancashire has retained the more rural and more attractive areas: the Ribble and Lune valleys, the Forest of Bowland, Pendle Hill, the Fylde and the West Pennine Moors as well as the limestone areas around Silverdale. The county will richly reward the walker who is prepared to explore the nooks and crannies, who is prepared to linger and who approaches it with an open mind. Both the major rivers, the Ribble and the Lune, rise high on the moorlands of the Yorkshire Dales to meander through the rich pastoral scenery of Lancashire to make their exits into the Irish Sea through wild, extensive and windswept mudflats or estuarine marshes which provide winter feeding grounds for hundreds of thousands of wading birds.

Other rivers such as the Hodder, the Wenning, the Yarrow and the Douglas twinkle and sparkle as they tumble from the hills so providing their own particular charm. The stone-built villages along the courses of all these rivers have a particular and individual character created by vernacular architecture. History is etched into their very stones. The villages are steeped in local traditions and folk-lore from the witches of Pendle to the Quakers of Bowland.

The landscape is peppered with pre-historic sites from Bronze-Age burial mounds to Celtic forts. Fine and imposing mansions with their extensive parklands add an extra dimension. A further facet of history is provided by the industrial relics which were the forerunners of the Industrial Revolution. These include the coppiced woodlands, the handloom weavers' cottages of Central Lancashire and the lime-kilns of Silverdale.

Although it may lack the towering mountains of Scotland, North Wales or the Lake District, Lancashire can offer upland scenery which is both breathtaking and attractive. Walking in the Forest of Bowland may prove both challenging and rewarding with spectacular views from the summits of Parlick, Fair Snape Fell and Nicky Nook.

In sharp contrast there are the gentler, rolling hills of the limestone areas around Silverdale and Warton and the lush riverside pastures of the valleys. Add to these long stretches of coastal paths and you have a variety which few other counties can offer.

Sadly, Lancashire does not boast a National Park although when David Trippier was Member of Parliament for Rossendale and Minister for the Countryside he actually advocated that status for the Forest of Bowland. Unfortunately, on the advice of the Countryside Commission and other bodies, he abandoned the idea. However, by then Bowland had already been designated an Area of Outstanding Natural Beauty (AONB). The Arnside and Silverdale areas, straddling the Lancashire-Cumbria boundary, also enjoy a similar designation which does afford a certain amount of protection.

Running north from Preston to the Cumbrian boundary the Lancaster Canal provides a linear route which contrasts sharply both in character and scenery with the high moorlands of the West Pennine Moors and the Forest of Bowland and with the coastal marshes fringing Morecambe Bay.

The City of Lancaster, dominated by its Castle, Priory Church and royal associations, is a maze of narrow alleys that can be explored only on foot. The preservation of the city's rich maritime history has bequeathed not only an excellent museum but also a magnificent water-front walk.

This variety of landscape provides ideal habitats for a mixture of wildlife ranging from the breeding birds of the uplands such as lapwing and golden plover to the wintering birds of the coastal marshes. The limestone areas around Silverdale support a summer flora that is the botanist's dream and this, in turn, attracts numerous species of butterfly. Add the occasional sightings of fox, stoat, weasel and hare and it is clear that a walk anywhere in the county is automatically bound to be full of interest.

Lancashire boasts scores of nature reserves owned and managed by the Lancashire Wildlife Trust. The Royal Society for the Protection of Birds has a very strong presence with major reserves at Hest Bank and Leighton Moss, the latter famous for its breeding marsh harriers, bitterns, bearded tits and wild otters.

It is this assortment of scenic views, historical remains and natural history that makes any walk in Lancashire more than worth the effort. It has something to offer walkers of all ages and capabilities from the serious fell walker to the afternoon stroller.

About the Walks

This collection of walks has been assembled to reveal the finest of Lancashire's countryside. Their distribution throughout the county, however, has been dictated, as the title of the book suggests, by the presence of tea rooms.

Most of the walks are short: few exceed five miles in length. They should be within the capability of most people and are eminently suitable for families with young children. Where there are special difficulties involving navigation or severe climbing notice is given in the text.

Road walking has been kept to a minimum, although it is occasionally necessary to link paths and so form a circular route. All the routes follow public rights of way as shown on the Ordnance Survey maps, whether they be public footpaths or bridleways. In a few instances concessionary paths have been included following the recent introduction of various access schemes by the Countryside Commission, the Forestry Commission, the privatised water companies or local authorities. Stretches of path that are less frequently used may be difficult to detect on the ground. Where this is the case, mention is made in the text and more detailed navigational instructions included.

There was a temptation to include ascents of such popular summits as Pendle Hill, Parlick and Wolf Fell but I have avoided these in the interests of conservation. Stand in Barley village, for instance, and you are immediately struck by the wide scar defacing the flank of Pendle. It is simply the result of too many pairs of walking boots causing erosion. I do not want to add to the problem by encouraging more people to pound the fragile surface.

Afternoon tea

Afternoon Tea is quintessentially English. The very mention of the phrase brings to mind images of wafer-thin cucumber sandwiches, stands of delectable scones, delicious cakes and cream accompanied by freshly-brewed tea served from an elegant silver pot. This idealised concept inspired several scenes in the plays of Oscar Wilde and prompted the poet Rupert Brooke to write:

"Stands the church clock at ten to three?
"And is there honey still for tea?"

Many hotels have developed Afternoon Tea into a social ritual held against a background of light music provided by a small ensemble.

The English obsession with tea was a direct consequence of the conquest of India and Ceylon by Robert Clive and other British Generals in the eighteenth century. Heavily promoted by the East India Company, it quickly ousted its main rivals, coffee and chocolate, which were often regarded as the preferred drinks of our enemies of the period, the French and the Spanish. Tea drinking was equated with patriotism. In recent years its leading position has been seriously challenged in this country by a revived interest in coffee but, so far, it has successfully resisted the threat.

Most English people will drink a cup of tea at any time of day on the flimsiest of excuses but late afternoon is still probably regarded as the favourite. To cater for this obsession, the country has developed a network of cafes, many of which are to be found in country villages. For reasons of viability they do not specialise in tea alone, but offer other beverages such as coffee, chocolate and soft drinks alongside cakes, scones and gateaux. Most, if not all, offer light snacks on their menu.

Everyone has their ideal vision of what a country café should be but, as in other walks of life, times change and tea shops with them. The cosy establishment with linen tablecloths and bone china may still be found but others are of the self-service variety. Whatever the type of tea room, the real criteria is that satisfying pot of tea accompanied by a cholesterol-defying cream cake.

Some of the cafes mentioned in this collection offer wide-ranging menus including full meals, while others provide snacks and similar refreshments depending on the time of day. For me, however, a pot of freshly-brewed tea served with equally fresh scones, jam and cream, is the best way to round-off a day's walk in the countryside.

The tea shops featured in this book are as varied as the scenery which they serve, each having its own ambience and atmosphere. One is housed in a massive cruck barn of Scandinavian origin, another is secreted down a narrow alley while a third forms part of an art gallery. One is to be found in a stately home, one in a butcher's shop and two in working post offices. Others occupy a former canal warehouse, a handloom weaver's cottage and a converted smithy.

The opening times listed for each tea room were correct at the time of writing, and were re-checked as late as possible. However, they may change. So, before embarking on your walk, it is advisable to check that nothing has changed. For this reason the telephone number has been included.

Note that some cafes close completely during the winter while others have a restricted week-end opening. In some cases cafes will close completely either because of the expiration of a lease or because the owners wish to retire from the business. Some may change owners with a consequent change of menu and style.

Please, as an act of courtesy and common sense, remove your muddy walking boots before entering. Many of the tea shops are luxuriously carpeted and do not exist to serve only walkers. Again, for the convenience of other patrons, you may be requested to leave your rucksack outside. Most proprietors welcome walkers and offer hospitality that has no equal anywhere else in the country.

Tourist information

Lancashire is rich with tourist attractions ranging from the massive Castle, Priory Church and Maritime Museum in Lancaster to several working farms which open their gates, and their stables, to the general public. Between these extremes come stately homes, small stone cottages with historical associations, pre-historical sites, Roman forts, 'Lost Villages', ancient packhorse bridges, abbeys and nature reserves.

References to many of these are included in the text of the individual walks but there is no space in a book of this type to provide detailed information. Small booklets and leaflets about most of the attractions are available at the local Tourist Information Centres which also sell souvenirs and Ordnance Survey maps.

For anyone wishing to stay for a few days these centres provide information about the various types of accommodation available in their particular areas ranging from four star hotels to farmhouse bed and breakfast and even camping barns. In addition they operate a booking service.

The Tourist Information Centres also deal with queries relating to bus and train services, church services, shopping facilities and local events. The principal Tourist Information Centres are to be found at:
Lancaster: 19, Castle Hill, LA1 1YN. Phone: 01524 32878.
Clitheroe: 12-14 Market Place, BB7 2DA. Phone: 01200 25566.
Rivington: Great House Barn. BL6 7SB. Phone: 01204 691549 (restricted service).

Clothing and equipment

Even on the shortest walk, good outdoor clothing will not only improve your safety but also enhance your enjoyment. Obviously clothing is often a matter of personal choice, but there are some general guidelines.

Jeans, for example, are not advisable in cold, wet, weather because they tend to increase the risk of hypothermia. Shorts are an acceptable part of the outdoor scene in hot weather but do increase the risk of sunburn if the legs are exposed to bright sunshine for too long. Most outdoor clothing shops offer a choice of walking trousers that are suitable for most conditions but do remember that thicker ones are advisable in the winter and in colder weather.

A good pair of walking boots or shoes is essential, even on lower ground where paths can be very muddy, especially after a period of rain. It is as easy to twist an ankle on a level riverside path as it is high in the mountains. Boots have the advantage of providing extra support for the ankles, especially on rocky or uneven ground. Any good stockist will offer a wide range to choose from at varying prices to suit your pocket and the type of walking you plan to do.

The heavier type of walking boot, so necessary for mountain walking, will not be necessary for this collection of routes. On the other hand, smart shoes with high heels or sandals are not recommended.

Remember that walking boots and shoes have specially designed treads to improve their grip in slippery conditions such as wet surfaces, ice or even grassy slopes. It is also suggested that you wear two pairs of walking socks, so allow for this when buying your boots. Most shops will provide two pairs during the fitting sessions.

Because the British climate is so fickle and variable wet weather gear is essential. In recent years considerable improvements have been made in the types of material available including 'Gore-Tex' and other 'breathable' fabrics. These tend to eliminate or reduce condensation. Again, a good stockist will offer advise on what is available in this field.

Because temperatures between the valley bottom and the fell top vary, it is advisable to carry an extra pullover in your rucksack. Clothing should not be too tightly fitting but reasonably loose and comfortable. The modern trend is to use 'Fleece' garments rather than woollen jumpers and there is now a wide range of lightweight but warm underwear on the market. In colder weather the extremities such as fingers and ears should be covered because it is from these that most heat loss occurs. A warm, woolly hat which has ear flaps or can be pulled down over the ears, is a must. So, too, are gloves.

Even on the shortest and lowest level of walk carry a first-aid kit. You are always at risk of minor cuts and bruises from barbed wire, bramble bushes and stone walls. Another useful item is a pocket knife. On most of these walks you are unlikely to encounter any major problems but, to call for assistance, a whistle is a useful tool.

Remember that these are suggestions. On a sunny, summer day, several of these short walks can be enjoyed without worrying too much about clothing as long as you wear a decent pair of boots or shoes.

Food, too, is a matter of personal taste but ensure that at all times you carry some form of emergency rations in the form of chocolate or nutty bars which will provide extra energy in case of delay.

To carry your essential equipment a good day sack of 25 or 35 litres should prove more than adequate. To ensure that your spare clothing, food and other equipment remains dry in wet weather, it is a good idea to line the inside of the rucksack with a plastic bag.

Transport

By car

Many people will travel to the start of each of these walks by car. For their benefit route directions have been given in the fact section at the beginning of each walk, along with details of parking facilities.

By rail

Preston and Lancaster are both served by the West Coast main line which runs between London and Glasgow. Both towns also have direct links with Blackburn, Bolton, Manchester and Manchester Airport. Lancaster has a direct service to Skipton and Leeds.

Clitheroe Station, originally closed in 1962, re-opened in 1994 and has frequent daily services to Blackburn, Bolton and Manchester Victoria. Silverdale is served by trains from Lancaster, Carnforth and Barrow-in-Furness.

From all these stations there are connecting buses to local towns and villages. Various points around Silverdale are served by the "Silverdale Shuttle" operating Mondays to Fridays. Up-to-date rail travel information may be obtained on the following telephone numbers:

Lancaster: 01524 32333
Preston: 01772 259439
Manchester: 0161 832 8353
Clitheroe: 01200 443800

By bus

Clitheroe, Lancaster, Preston and Garstang are linked by express bus services to London, Manchester and other major towns. They are also at the hub of the local bus network. Some towns and villages still enjoy the benefit of a frequent daily bus service, including Sundays, but others have to rely on the occasional bus, perhaps on a local market day. Many of the more remote areas are served by special recreational buses which operate from local towns only on Summer Sundays and Bank Holidays.

Details of all available services are provided at the beginning of each route description. Although these were correct at the time of going to press it is advisable to remember that since de-Regulation, bus and train services are subject to change at very short notice. Therefore, it is essential to check before setting out for your walk. To facilitate this the telephone numbers of Bus Information Centres are given below.

Accrington: 01254 872595
Blackburn: 01254 681120
Blackpool: 01253 751485
Burnley: 01282 423125
Clitheroe: 01200 442226
Fleetwood: 01253 772704
Lancaster: 01524 841656
Nelson: 01282 698533
Preston: 01772 556618

Maps

All the routes in this collection were devised and walked using the Ordnance Survey's 1:25 000 series of "Pathfinder" maps. However, this series of maps will gradually be phased out. For much of Lancashire it has been replaced by "The Forest of Bowland and Ribblesdale", number 41 in the "Outdoor Leisure" series at the same scale, 1:25 000. Where relevant, I have quoted this map. Otherwise, at present, there is no alternative but to refer to the "Pathfinder" series.

Walk 1: Rivington

Using field paths and bridleways this route traverses parkland, upland pastures and open moorland whilst offering superb views over the central Lancashire plain.

Route: Great House Barn – Rivington Hall – Lower House – Old Rachel's – Willcock's Farm – Yarrow Reservoir – Dean Wood – Rivington village – Great House Barn.

Start: Great House Barn, Rivington Lane, Rivington. Map reference 629139.

Distance: 4¾ miles (7.5km)

Map: Bolton (North) and Horwich", number 700 in the O.S. "Pathfinder" series.

Public Transport: In summer there is a daily bus service from Leigh to the Great House Barn. This stops at the Crown Hotel, Horwich, to meet connections from Bolton and other local towns. In winter there is a Sunday service only.

By Car: To reach Great House Barn leave the M61 at Junction 6. Follow the A6027 to its junction with the A673 at the southern approach to Horwich. Turn left along the A673. On the northern outskirts of Horwich turn right into Lever Park Avenue (signed to Rivington). This develops into Rivington Lane before reaching the Great House Barn which is on the left. There is a large car park. From Bolton follow the A673 to Horwich and then proceed as above.

The Tea Shop

Light refreshments are available in Great House Barn, a large but simple building dominated by its black and white interior and enormous cruck frames constructed of solid oak. The cafeteria service offers soup of the day, toasted sandwiches, filled jacket potatoes, scones, fruit pies, cakes and cream gateaux along with ice cream, soft drinks and freshly-brewed tea and coffee.

The Great House Barn also houses an Information Centre where leaflets and books on various aspects of the West Pennine Moors may be purchased. There are also changing exhibitions about the area. **Opening Times:** 10.30am to 5pm daily, all year. Closed Christmas Day. **Phone:** 01204 691549

Rivington

The collection of reservoirs in Rivington and Anglezarke, set amongst dramatic rolling moorlands, has led to this district being dubbed "The Lancashire Lakeland". It lies on the south western edge of the West Pennine Moors, an area managed for informal recreation by North West Water PLC, Lancashire County Council, Bolton Metropolitan Borough Council and Bury Metropolitan Borough Council.

Records reveal that the Rivington Hall Estate of 2, 100 acres passed through several owners until it was bought by Lord Leverhulme in 1899. A native of nearby Bolton, who had amassed a fortune by producing and selling "Sunlight" soap, Leverhulme retained a mere 45 acres for his private use whilst donating the remainder to the people of Bolton for use as a country park, an enlightened concept well in advance of its time.

Between 1902 and 1905 he fought a protracted legal battle against Liverpool Corporation which sought control of the land which fed its reservoirs. This dispute was finally settled by a Select Committee of the House of Commons which decided that Liverpool should buy the estate, although at double the price Leverhulme had paid for it. With a sense of irony the Select Committee decreed that the park should be known as "Lever Park" and should remain part of the public domain as Lord Leverhulme had originally intended.

On the private part of the estate Lord Leverhulme challenged nature by creating a large area of terraced gardens out of the moorlands which were planted with rhododendrons and other exotic species. One of the highlights was the Japanese Garden with its ponds, fountains, pathways and ornamental structures.

He also built a bungalow, later destroyed by fire, from where it is reputed he could observe the smoking chimneys of his factory at Port Sunlight on the Wirral. There were also several follies including the Dovecote, now a prominent landmark, and the pseudo ruins of Liverpool Castle.

Following his death the gardens were neglected and became so overgrown that they were almost impossible to penetrate. In the 1970s, funded by North West Water, the British Trust for Conservation Volunteers opened-up the paths and restored the gardens to their former glory.

The Barns

The two barns at Rivington are regarded as two of the finest examples of the cruck type of construction still standing in this country. The Hall Barn, as its name suggests, served the Hall while Great House Barn was

Great House Barn

adjacent to the two storey building with a stone slated roof and mullioned windows which was formerly Great House Farm. This has been converted into a Ranger's Office, Art Gallery and Toilet Block. The two barns, approximately half a mile apart, are linked by a splendid tree-lined avenue known as Hall Drive.

The exact age of the two barns has become a matter of controversy. Some scholars suggest that they were built originally in the Viking period because similar types have been discovered in Scandinavia but most of the present buildings date from the early eighteenth century. During the winter months they were used for housing livestock as well as storing feed. Lord Leverhulme had them adapted and opened as places of refreshment serving his country park.

Leaflets describing the methods of construction of these cruck-framed barns may be obtained from the Information Centre housed in the Great House Barn. **Opening Times:** 10.30am to 5pm daily, all year. Closed Christmas Day.

The Route

Leave the car park to the left of the Great House Barn before crossing directly over Rivington Lane to walk along Hall Drive as it runs through some magnificent parkland. The drive is surfaced but, fortunately, there is a good grassy path running alongside.

After approximately 250 metres, facing the elegant red brick Georgian Hall and by a large sign directing traffic for Hall Barn to the left, turn right along a wide track signed as part of the Terraced Garden Trail.

Within 50 metres make a sharp turn to the right onto another wide track which, according to the sign, is the next section of the Terraced Garden Trail. The Hall is now on the left with woodlands on the right. After a very short distance a low drystone wall appears, also on the left.

On arriving at a junction in front of a stone cottage initially go left but, almost immediately turn right, thereby passing to the left of the cottage and walking for one hundred metres towards a large wooden gate bearing a blue waymarker arrow.

Beyond this gate maintain direction along a fenced bridleway, climbing gently beside the stream on your right until, following a slight dip, a T-junction is reached. Turn left to climb for some 20 metres before making a right turn to a waymarked, wooden ladder stile.

Immediately over this turn sharp left, keeping just to the right of a fence until gaining another stile. Make another left turn to head across a short stretch of duckboarding and then directly over the field for 100 metres to a stile which is both obvious and has a bridleway sign adjacent.

This stile provides access to a small car park at Lower House. Ignore two bridleways leading off to the right. Instead, staying to the right of the car park, proceed directly forward along a surfaced road to negotiate a waymarked traffic barrier. Where the road bends sharply round to the left to enter a second parking lot, stay forward along a narrow footpath to gain a waymarked stile within 20 metres.

The new path climbs gradually over grassland that has been wellcropped by sheep. To the right the entire stretch is dominated by the steep, brooding mass of Catter Nab, an outlier of Rivington Moor.

From the stile, as the path is somewhat vague, head for the obvious waymarker post some distance ahead which, in turn, is followed by a second. Maintain direction over two separate sets of duckboarding to a ladder stile allowing access to a small conifer plantation.

Cross a small wooden footbridge, negotiate another stile and having left the plantation, proceed across open upland grazing to a further marker post.

From there start the descent into a small moorland clough with its

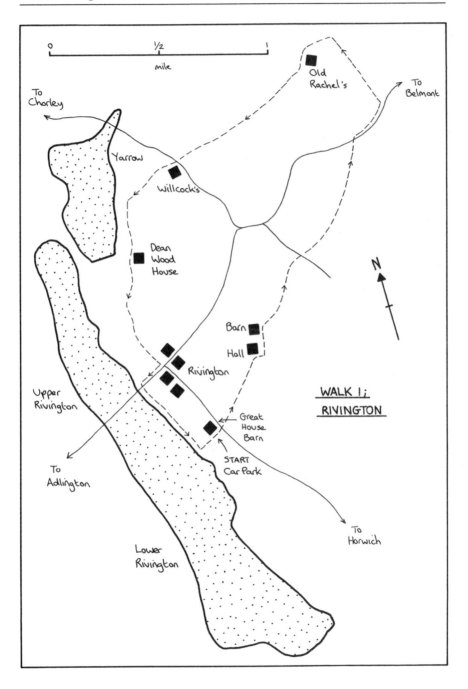

WALK 1;
RIVINGTON

typical shale flanks to cross more duckboards to a stile. Turn right for a few metres before swinging left over a footbridge.

At the far end turn left again to reach a stile which is followed immediately by a climb up a very short flight of steps. From the top stay to the left of a fence until a stile provides an exit onto Belmont Road.

Turn right and, exercising extreme caution round a couple of tight bends, head in the direction of Belmont. After 300 metres turn left off the unfenced road onto a wide track which leads, after 20 metres, to a waymarked stone step stile. This is set into a drystone wall adjacent to a new five-barred metal gate.

From a height of 300 metres this spot offers a panoramic view over the shallow moorland basin of the infant River Yarrow, bounded on the right by Spitler's Edge and Redmond's Edge as they head towards the summit of Great Hill at 381 metres. To the left the moorlands fall away to the Central Lancashire Plain while behind stand the T.V. transmitters of Winter Hill.

From the stile and losing height very gradually, walk away from the road in a straight line over open moorland, as the path goes towards a waymarker post with two arrows. Continue in the same direction for a further 100 metres to a footpath sign with three arms.

There turn left along another broad track with the River Yarrow, little more than a stream at this point, a short distance away to the right. The track leads down the shallow valley, passing through extensive areas of reeds and moorland grass.

Beyond the first waymarker post stay to the immediate right of the ruins of Old Rachel's Farm, emptied of both people and stock because it was located on the water-gathering grounds of the reservoirs in the distant valleys below.

Keep to the same line of direction, guided by two further waymarker posts, until reaching a sign with three arms. Stay forward for a few metres, advancing to the left of a wall to negotiate a stile. Immediately turn right over a second stile and, almost at once, turn left to proceed with a barbed wire fence and a derelict wall on your right.

Guided by the next waymarker post, remain with the distinct path as it continues along the same line of direction whilst traversing rough pasture peppered with reeds and molehills. As a further guide there is a wire fence and a ditch on the left.

Where the fence reaches a corner with yet another waymarker post adjacent, make a left turn through a metal five-barred gate before making a right turn. In crossing the next field veer slightly towards the left whilst aiming for the tall ladder stile a few metres to the right of Wilcock's Farm which stands by the road to Anglezarke.

Turn right along the road but, having negotiated the first bend, make a left turn by a wall corner to walk over a small patch of waste ground to a waymarked stile. Head marginally leftwards whilst staying to the right of the occasional wind-blown hawthorn, crossing the field directly to another stile.

Continue forwards for some 50 metres to meet another path which forms a T-junction.

Turn left and, with Yarrow Reservoir a short distance away on your right, follow a succession of waymarker posts. Eventually the path meets and runs alongside a wall until, a few metres beyond the embankment, it drops down the slope to a stile. Beyond this the path develops into a wide track as it twists and turns by the entrance to Dean Wood House and acquires a line of rhododendrons on each side.

A few metres beyond a green metal kissing gate, adjacent to a five-barred one, turn left over a stile to walk through the wood and alongside a stream where, even in winter the blue tits, great tits, robins and blackbirds announce their presence.

After negotiating a through stile, climb a flight of steps adjacent to a cascading stream before crossing a small field to a wooden kissing gate and Sheephouse Lane.

Turn right for 50 metres to Rivington village green and a road junction. To the left is one of the oldest Unitarian Chapels in England. The Congregation was founded shortly after the lifting of anti-Puritan legislation in 1662 and the present building, still in regular use, dates from 1703.

At the road junction stay forward in the direction signed to Adlington and Chorley but, after 100 metres, and by the village school, swing left onto a bridleway. Lower Rivington Reservoir is on your right.

By a small car park, where the bridleway curves round to the left, stay forward through a set of wooden posts onto another bridleway which runs through the trees alongside the reservoir. After a short distance this, too, bends round to the left to enter the car park by Great House Barn.

Walk 2: Rufford

An easy walk through the drained marshlands and meres of West
Lancashire where the hills of the West Pennine Moors form but a distant
backcloth. It is a landscape of extensive vistas, reminiscent of the
Fenlands of East Anglia where arable farming reigns supreme.

Route: Rufford Old Hall – Leeds and Liverpool Canal – Mere Lane –
Cousins Lane – Rufford Boundary Sluice – Mere Sands Wood – Park
Farm – Spark Bridge – Rufford Old Hall.

Start: Rufford Old Hall. Map reference 464160.

Distance: 5 miles (8km).

Map: "Chorley and Burscough Bridge", number 699 in the O.S. "Pathfinder"
series.

Public Transport: The Stagecoach-Ribble and North-Western service number 101,
Ormskirk to Preston, stops at the entrance. So do Blackpool
Transport's numbers 754/758 Blackpool to Liverpool service. All these
services operate seven days a week. Rufford Station is served by
frequent trains from Ormskirk and Preston except on Sundays.
Connections at Ormskirk for Liverpool.

By Car: Rufford Old Hall (signed) is on the A59, Liverpool to Preston trunk road.
It is located in the village of Rufford some 2½ miles north of
Burscough Bridge. There is a car park where a small fee is charged.

The Tea Shop

The Tea Rooms at Rufford Old Hall are located in the former stables
block. With their plain wooden doors and stone flagged floors they have
managed to retain the atmosphere of yesteryear. Appropriately the walls
are decorated with an assortment of large pewter plates and dishes,
old-fashioned kitchen utensils and willow-patterned crockery.

"Beef Cobbler", "Gardener's Lunch" and "Traditional Rarebit" are
amongst the unusual items featured on the menu but, if these fail to
tempt your imagination or your palate, there is a bewildering selection
of salads and jacket potatoes on offer.

For anyone finishing the walk during the afternoon there is even a
choice of Afternoon Teas, not to mention a tempting array of mouth-

watering scones, cakes and ice creams. The thirsty may choose from several speciality teas, coffees or wines including gooseberry and elder.

Opening Times: Daily, 1st April to 30th October: 12.00am to 5.00pm.(Last orders 4.30pm.) Closed Thursday and Friday; 2nd November to 19th December: Daily 12.00am to 4.00pm. Closed Monday and Friday. There is an admission charge to the Hall and Gardens except for National Trust members. **Phone:** 01704 821254

Rufford Old Hall

Rufford Old Hall is one of the architectural gems of Lancashire. Surprisingly, it is also one of the few properties in the county owned by the National Trust. It was donated to this body in 1936 by Lord Hesketh and, with its partial black and white exterior, is reckoned to be one of the finest sixteenth century buildings in Lancashire.

The Old Hall was probably constructed by Sir Robert Hesketh, Lord of the Manor, at some date between 1523 and 1541. The family was amongst the wealthiest and most powerful in the area and Sir Thomas Hesketh maintained a company of actors amongst whom, according to tradition at least, was the young William Shakespeare.

The Hall originally had two wings, but the timber-framed West Wing

The Old Hall

was demolished to be replaced by a new brick building in 1662 to accommodate both family and servants. In the 1760s the family moved to Rufford New Hall but the Old Hall was occupied in the 1820s by Sir Thomas Henry Hesketh, eldest son of the third Baronet.

The interior of the Great Hall, still maintained in its original condition, is famous for its beautifully carved movable screen and hammer beam roof. The carved canopy at one end of the hall conceals the entrance to a secret chamber. Today there is a fine display of furniture, weaponry and armour. Other rooms open to the public include the Dining Room, Study, Schoolroom, Drawing Room and Bedroom. The formal gardens and woodlands cover eighteen acres.

Mere Sands Wood

Mere Sands Wood is a nature reserve covering 44 hectares of heathland, woodland and lakes in the heart of West Lancashire's agricultural belt. Owned by the Lancashire Wildlife Trust since 1982, it was formally declared a Site of Special Scientific Interest because of its geological interest. It occupies an area of layered peat and sand laid down over boulder clay during the last Ice Age and has remained undisturbed ever since.

The woodlands consist mainly of birch and oak, but one section of Scots Pines is home to a small population of Red Squirrel, one of the few remaining pockets of our native species in England. Mere Sands Wood is also noted for the Broad Buckler Fern, Dog Violet, Bluebell and Foxglove while in early Spring it is carpeted with Wild Garlic and Wood Anemone. It boasts four species of Orchid – Common Spotted, Early Marsh, Spotted Marsh and Bee.

The Route

Leave the grounds of Rufford Old Hall by the main entrance onto the A59. Turn left along the pavement, walking towards Rufford village. After approximately 1km, turn left into Diamond Jubilee Lane, the B5246, which is signed to the railway station and Parbold.

Soon you pass to the right of St Mary's parish church, a red brick edifice and, some 50 metres beyond, reach the canal bridge with its green metal railings. At the far end of this bridge turn sharply to the right and onto the towpath of the Leeds and Liverpool Canal.

Continue along this with its soft, grassy surface, first passing to the right of a metal barrier and, a little later, a set of locks. In summer the banks are lined with anglers whilst swallows dart and swerve overhead

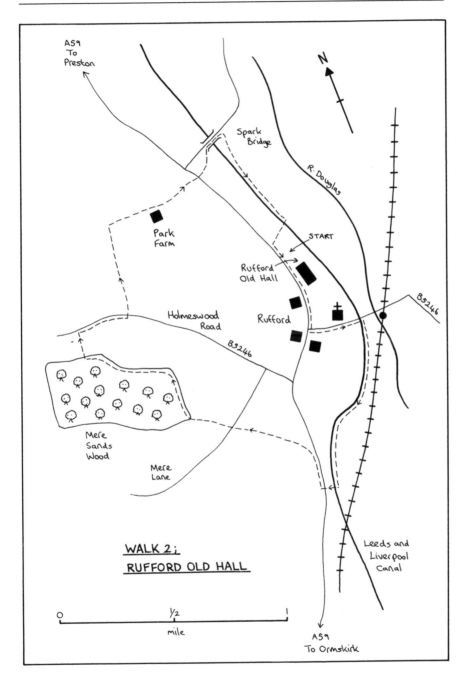

A59
To
Preston

N

Spark
Bridge

R. Douglas

Park
Farm

START

Rufford
Old Hall

Rufford

Holmeswood
Road

B5246

B5246

Mere
Sands
Wood

Mere
Lane

Leeds and
Liverpool
Canal

WALK 2;
RUFFORD OLD HALL

0   ½   1
mile

A59
To Ormskirk

as they hawk for flying insects. The edges of the water are lined with a mixture reeds, yellow flag and water lilies.

After running very close to the railway for a short distance the canal arcs round towards the right whilst the vast expanse of Marsh Moss occupies the ground to your left.

Pass through a large white metal gate which straddles the towpath and immediately turn right over a swing bridge to gain the A59.

Exercising extreme caution because this is a very busy trunk road, cross to the pavement on the opposite side and turn right along it, reaching the 40 MPH signs after a mere 20 metres. 10 metres further, at the near end of a bridge and by a footpath sign, turn left to walk 5 metres to a wide cinder track. Turn right along this to arrive at a Y-junction after 100 metres. Fork left, so keeping some farm buildings on your right.

The adjacent field is laid out in a peculiar fashion with notices which read "Exit". Ignore all these. Continue to a T-junction. Turn left for 10 metres and then turn right to pass a white Portakabin. Cross over a tiny stone bridge with metal railings and, at the far end and by another footpath sign, make a left turn to walk a very narrow footpath which squeezes its course between a tall hawthorn hedge on the right and a narrow stream, the Rufford Boundary Sluice, on the left.

At this point there is an extensive panorama over the fertile land created several centuries ago by the draining of the original Martin Mere. In the far distance Southport is clearly visible.

The narrow path finally emerges onto Mere Lane by a footpath sign and the Rufford Centre which is owned by the Ormskirk Methodist Church. Turn left along the surfaced road and, having crossed another narrow bridge spanning the Rufford Boundary Sluice, turn right as indicated by a footpath sign to continue along another path, this time with the stream on your right and some houses on your left.

It leads to Cousins Lane. Cross this directly to walk a wide track which runs alongside Rufford Cricket Ground. Beyond the newly-built pavilion the track narrows into a path which maintains direction along the boundary of an arable field until reaching a wooden kissing gate which permits entry into Mere Sands Wood.

Immediately through the gate make a ninety degree turn to the right to follow the well maintained path which stays just inside the wood albeit close to the reserve boundary.

At this stage of the walk the trees are mainly birch and oak with an under-storey of bramble, ferns and rhododendron which create an admirable habitat for the blackbirds, titmice of several species, robins and jays which invariably rise at the sound of approaching footsteps.

After approximately 1km the path forms a T-junction with the entrance drive to the nature reserve. To call at the Visitor Centre with its interesting exhibitions, turn left for a few metres. Otherwise, make a right turn along the driveway itself for the 200 metres to Holmeswood Road.

Turn right, and using the pavement, proceed for 200 metres to meet a bridleway sign. Ignoring a notice which reads, "Private Road", turn left to walk along this bridleway with the woodlands of Rufford Park on your right. There is another extensive expanse of mossland to your left.

After 500 metres the woodland terminates but, at a junction and by a "Riding Prohibited" sign, swing through ninety degrees to the right. Within a few hundred metres pass between the buildings of Park Farm from which emanates a strangè, eerie atmosphere created by the mainly derelict buildings.

Beyond, the wide track passes through more arable fields with Winter Hill and Great Hill in the far distance ahead. Eventually the track reaches the A59. Cross directly into Spark Lane and follow it for some 300 metres until it climbs ever so slightly to form a T-junction with the A581 by Spark Bridge.

Turn right over the bridge but, at the far end, turn left down a flight of concrete steps onto the towpath of the Leeds and Liverpool Canal. At the foot of the steps turn left, pass under the bridge, and continue along the towpath for 1km. Turn right across the black and white swing bridge and proceed down the subsequent lane until reaching the A59 once again. Turn left to walk along the pavement for the final 250 metres to the entrance to Rufford Old Hall.

Walk 3: Wycoller

A pleasant walk starting from Wycoller Country Park to follow field and moorland paths with some excellent wide-ranging views over the upland landscape.

Route: Trawden Road car park – Wycoller – Clam Bridge – Bank House – Viewpoint Rocks – Raven's Rock Farm – Wycoller – Trawden Road car park.

Start: Trawden Road car park. Map reference 926395.

Distance: 4½ miles (7km)

Map: "South Pennines", number 21 in the O.S. "Outdoor Leisure" series.

Public Transport: None direct. The only bus service is number 25 from Burnley, Nelson and Colne to Laneshaw Bridge which is one and a half miles from Wycoller.

By car: From the end of the M65 follow the A6068 signed to Keighley through Colne. At the junction with the A56, Skipton Road, (traffic lights), stay forward to the first traffic island. There, turn right to follow the signs to Wycoller Country Park via Trawden.

The Tea Shop

Approached through the Craft Shop, the Tea Rooms at Wycoller are housed in an old stone cottage which is festooned with flowers during the summer months. Everything is in keeping with the ambience of the village itself. The beamed white ceiling is mirrored by the stone flagged floors and the exposed stonework is decorated with prints and photos. There is an unusual stone column in the centre, a traditional York Range and a Welsh style dresser housing a display of traditional plates. The tables are covered with Burgundy and lace tablecloths so creating a very cosy atmosphere especially on those cold, wet days so frequent in the Pennines. For the hot, sunny days of summer there are tables outside.

The menu is equally simple and includes such snacks as Ravioli on Toast and Beans on Toast along with sandwiches, both plain and toasted. For anyone with a more substantial appetite there is a selection from Pie and Peas, Ploughman's Lunch and Farrier's Lunch, all served with salads.

For that afternoon treat there is a mouth-watering selection of home-made scones with cream, gateaux and cakes, all oozing cream, to be followed by a freshly brewed pot of tea or coffee. **Opening Times:** 11am to 5pm daily except Mondays all year round. **Phone:** 01282 868395.

Wycoller

Like Lazarus, Wycoller died but returned to life. Clustered around the ruins of its Hall and aisled barn, it is one of the most attractive and fascinating places in Lancashire today. However, a few decades ago it almost disappeared off the map and its resurrection is one of the miracles of modern conservation.

Several unique aspects of its long history have survived to make a visit worthwhile, even without any walking in the glorious countryside in which it is cradled. The settlement in this once-remote upland valley pre-dates the Norman Conquest of 1066 and its Saxon name means, "Dairy Farm Among the Alders".

It remained an undistinguished farming hamlet until the eighteenth century when the development of the handloom weaving industry brought unexpected prosperity to the farmers who had previously eked out a precarious living. The Hall was built in the sixteenth century by the Hartley family but was considerably extended and improved in the

Clapper bridge, Wycoller

eighteenth by Squire Henry Owen Cunliffe in his bid to attract a wealthy wife. The effort left his finances over-stretched and when he died in 1818 he left considerable debts from which his family never recovered.

By 1900 the Hall stood deserted and neglected, much of its stonework plundered for use in buildings elsewhere. A notable visitor to Wycoller Hall was Charlotte Brontë who walked there from nearby Haworth. She employed it as the model of Ferndean Manor in her novel "Jane Eyre. Even today the ruins, now preserved, are considerable.

Towards the close of the nineteenth century a proposal was made for a reservoir in the Wycoller Valley by constructing a dam across Wycoller Brook. This scheme was eventually abandoned but the land remained in the ownership of the Water Board until 1973 when it was sold to Lancashire County Council for use as a country park. The village itself was declared to be a conservation area. To keep it clear of traffic, except for the handful of residents, two car parks have been created, one on the Trawden Road and the second on the Haworth Road.

The Aisled Barn dates from 1630 and is typical of its period in that it could be used for storing the larger amounts of crops as cereal prices spiralled, so making it economical to cultivate marginal land. This type of barn replaced the former cruck type such as those at Rivington. In later years the barn at Wycoller experienced several changes of usage from sheltering cattle to being employed as a coach house.

Wycoller Brook is spanned by several unusual bridges. The most primitive is the Clam, a single slab of stone believed to be more than a thousand years old. In the centre of the village is the twin-arched packhorse bridge and, nearby, one of the Clapper bridges – stone slabs supported by plain stone pillars.

The Aisled Barn has been adapted for use as an Information Centre where it is possible to buy several books and leaflets on the fascinating history and remains of this most unusual village.

The Route

Leave the Trawden Road car park by taking the path from the far end which is signed to "The Village". It runs alongside the road from which it is separated by a hedgerow for most of the way.

Where it does emerge onto the metalled road continue in the same direction until reaching the village. Pass the café on your left, cross the packhorse bridge, and stay to the right of the Information Centre and the ruins of Wycoller Hall.

Stay with this narrow road which is flanked by foxgloves in summer and has Wycoller Brook trickling by on the right. On reaching a ford on your right, turn right over the sloping Clam Bridge alongside to reach a

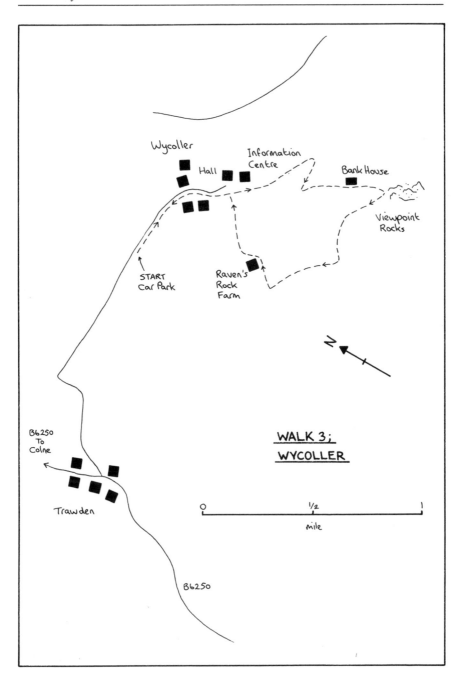

Wycoller

Hall

Information Centre

Bank House

Viewpoint Rocks

START Car Park

Raven's Rock Farm

N

B6250 To Colne

WALK 3; WYCOLLER

Trawden

0   ½   1

mile

B6250

waymarked stile. Climb with the track which bends round to the left after approximately 100 metres to a waymarker post.

Swing right, as directed, heading up the slope in a straight line by another waymarker post to reach a gateway. Through this turn left and, following the contour for a short distance, proceed towards Bank House with a small wood on your right.

A short distance before reaching the building and by the corner of a plantation, veer slightly towards the right and follow a series of way-markers keeping the house on your left. Remain with the track, as it resumes climbing but, by a small oblong stone embedded in the ground, fork left with the main track as it levels along the contour to a way-marked wooden five-barred gate with a stile adjacent.

Directed by yet another waymark, which indicates a viewpoint, negotiate the stile and advance for 100 metres to Viewpoint Rocks. This name is more than appropriate for from the rocks there is an extensive panorama out over the valley and surrounding uplands including Boulsworth Hill.

By the stones turn right following a fairly vague path as it ascends the moor diagonally to a wooden five-barred gate in a wire fence. Do not go through. Instead, turn left for a short distance and, 2 metres beyond the fence corner, turn right, heading towards a small wooden post some 50 metres directly ahead. The moorland is carpeted with cotton grass while the skylarks sing, a perfect accompaniment to some fine upland walking.

Continue in the same direction to pass through a waymarked gateway and stay a shade to the right of a stone wall until reaching a stone step stile some 10 metres to the left of the wall corner.

Beyond this follow the wall on your left as it corners eventually to a facing stile. Remain to the right of the wall to another step stile in the next field corner and then maintain the same line of direction to another stile, this time adjacent to a metal five-barred gate.

Over this turn right through ninety degrees, so walking to the left of the wall which subsequently gives way to a fence. Pass through a gateway and ignore the first stile on your right.

Continue to a second, which is waymarked. Turn right over this and head for the right-hand corner of Raven Rocks Farm which lies directly ahead.

Over the waymarked stile by the corner of the farm buildings, make a left turn along the track, pass by the farm buildings, and continue to lose height rapidly as you descend into the Wycoller Valley, emerging opposite to the ruins of the Hall.

Turn left for the Tea Rooms and, after refreshments, retrace your steps to the car park in Trawden Road.

Walk 4: Foulridge

A gentle rural walk along canal towpaths and field paths with clear views of the surrounding hills and countryside ranging as far as the Yorkshire Dales.

Route: Foulridge Wharf – Dauber's Bridge – Mill Hill Bridge – Dauber's – Foulridge Wharf.

Start: Canal Wharf, Foulridge. Map reference 888425.

Distance: 2¾ miles (4.5km).

Map: "The South Pennines", number 21 in the O.S. "Outdoor Leisure" series.

Public Transport: Foulridge is served by frequent daily buses (including Sundays) from Colne, Nelson, Burnley and Skipton. Many of these connect with the railway stations at Colne and Skipton. In Foulridge alight at the village Post Office.

By car: Foulridge is situated on the A56, Colne to Skipton road. To reach the Wharf (car park) follow the signs from the village centre.

The Tea Shop

The Tea Rooms are housed in the former Wharfmaster's Office and the stables once used to accommodate the barge horses. The stonework, brickwork and wooden beams provide the authentic aura of the period in which the Wharf was built, 1815. The lights are suspended from a genuine cartwheel which itself hangs by thick chains attached to the roof beams.

Not surprisingly, the walls are decorated with assorted memorabilia of the canal era. These are matched by the check table cloths, antique dresser and settle and a variety of chairs. There is also a cavernous stone fireplace where, in winter, a fire burns brightly in the grid-iron basket.

The menu is comprehensive ranging from a large variety of cooked meals to sandwiches and including home-made scones, cakes and gateaux, many served with a superfluity of cream. Few tea rooms anywhere, let alone in Lancashire, offer ten varieties of scone as they do in Foulridge.

Opening Times: Summer: daily, including Sundays, 10am to 6pm. Winter: daily 10am to dusk. Closed Mondays and Tuesdays. **Phone:** 01282 844033.

Foulridge

Prior to the construction of the Leeds and Liverpool Canal Foulridge was nothing more than a small, insignificant farming community, indistinguishable from dozens of others throughout the Pennine districts of Lancashire. However, it owes its present fame to the trans-Pennine waterway because it boasts a large, barn-like warehouse on the Wharf which was built in 1815, a year before the official opening of the canal in its entirety. During its heyday in the nineteenth century Foulridge Wharf was a bustle of activity as cargoes of cotton from the United States of America were unloaded there to be distributed to the local mills. Subsequently, bales of finished cotton cloth were loaded onto the barges for despatch to all four corners of the world.

Sadly this trade has vanished, along with all the other general cargoes that were once handled by this thriving inland port. Today pleasure cruises operate from the Wharf which is also a favourite mooring stop for people cruising the canal.

Foulridge Tunnel, opened in 1796, is a shade under 1,500 metres in length which make it the longest canal tunnel in the county. In the absence of a towpath through it, the bargees had to "leg" their boats through, a system which involved the men lying on their backs and pushing their feet against the walls. In 1880 this method was abandoned

On the Leeds-Liverpool canal

in favour of the use of a steam tug and traffic lights were installed to regulate the flow of traffic.

A most bizarre event occurred in 1912 when a cow named "Buttercup" fell into the canal at the Barrowford entrance to the tunnel. Allegedly she swam through to the Foulridge entrance where she was revived with alcohol. If you think this is something of a tall story then visit the "Hole in the Wall" pub where a photograph of this extraordinary beast is on display.

The Peel Mill stands on Warehouse Lane, which is used towards the end of this walk. Built in 1855, it was the first mill to appear in Foulridge and resulted in a population explosion in the village as workers poured in from far and wide. To cater for these the rows of terraced houses, many of which still stand, were built and so transformed the appearance of the village.

The Route

From the eastern end of the Wharf take the footpath which runs for a mere 10 metres towards a lime kiln which is dated 1790 to 1796. This was used for burning the lime used in the construction of the canal.

Advance a further 15 metres to join the canal towpath and turn right, so that the canal itself is on your left with pastures and the more distant moorlands away to your right.

Pass under the stone-arched Dauber's Bridge followed, subsequently, by the white-edged Hollinhurst Bridge as you walk one of the prettiest stretches of the whole length of the Leeds and Liverpool. In high summer there is a constant buzz of insects attracted by the bramble, harebells and other wild flowers lining the route.

On approaching the third bridge, Mill Hill, look for the triangular upright milestone in the form of a giant white Toblerone. It indicates a distance of 83 miles from Liverpool and 44½ from Leeds.

Take the steps to the right of Mill Hill Bridge and, at the top, make a left turn along the cobbled lane. At the far end of the bridge fork right through a metal five-barred gate to walk a rough track as it climbs gently to pass to the immediate right of a farm. There is a textile mill approximately 100 metres to your right. Emerge onto a lane facing four substantial stone houses.

Turn left along this lane and pass to the right of a white farm house. By the far corner of this make a right turn through a wooden five-barred gate and stay along the track as it climbs to a second. Continue up the slope whist veering very gradually towards a wall on the left.

On gaining the crown of the field turn left over a stone step stile to cross the centre of the subsequent field to another stone step stile. Beyond, cling close to the hedge on the right until reaching a third stone step stile about half way along the length of the field.

Turn right over this and then sharp left, so maintaining direction but now with the hedge on your left. Negotiate a squeezer stile in the facing wall to cross a very narrow field to a wooden stile and then maintain the same direction to a hybrid stile that is partially of the traditional wooden variety and partially a squeezer.

Beyond this continue forwards down the slope to the left of a stone wall to reach a somewhat obscured stile in the right-hand field corner. Pass under some overhead wires and cross a planked footbridge before veering left up a sloping field on a clear path to a stone squeezer stile flanked by two enormous holly trees which can prove to be very prickly to the unwary.

Make a bee-line across the next field to a squeezer stile, go directly over a green lane to another stile, and then proceed along the bottom boundary of a field which slopes upwards to your right. Stay to the right of Dauber's Farm to a step stile which affords access onto a lane. Turn right, climbing steeply until arriving almost but not quite at a minor road by a row of cottages.

A few metres before the junction with the road make a left turn through a squeezer stile adjacent to a wooden five-barred gate and a footpath sign. Aim for the boundary corner behind a bungalow and then continue along the same line for a further 50 metres to another stile. Foulridge Reservoir is now in view away to the right.

Beyond the stile stay forward around the base of a small, stone-covered hillock before swinging round to the left and losing further height to meet a stone wall coming in from the right. Turn right through a squeezer stile in this wall before descending a small flight of steps and crossing directly over a narrow surfaced track to a footpath sign with a wooden stile adjacent.

Continue in the same direction immediately to the right of a stone wall, pass through a gateway and, some 15 metres afterwards, veer left by a wall corner.

The subsequent field path is clear and easy to follow as it veers diagonally to the left, losing altitude to another stile, also of the squeezer variety. Turn right and remain to the left of a wall to yet another stile with a footpath sign alongside.

Stay forward over a cattle grid after 10 metres and remain along the lane until it reaches an open space. Veer leftwards between the houses onto Station Road and proceed to the far end. By the newsagent's on the corner, make a left turn into Warehouse Lane for the final 200 metres to Foulridge Wharf and that magnificent selection of scones.

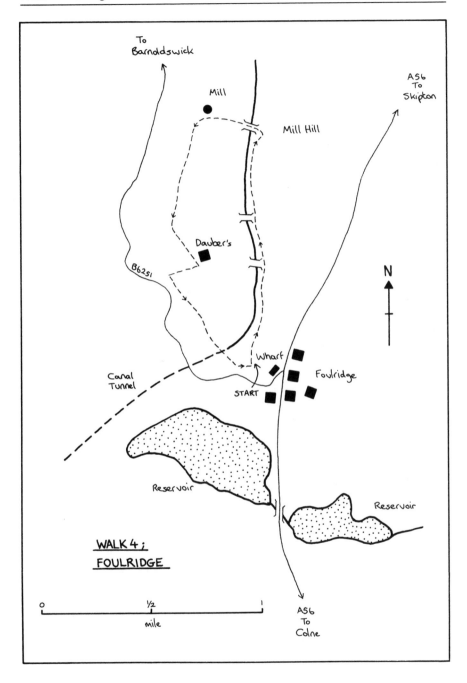

To
Barnoldswick

Mill

Mill Hill

A56
To
Skipton

Dauber's

B6251

N

Canal
Tunnel

Wharf

START

Foulridge

Reservoir

Reservoir

WALK 4;
FOULRIDGE

0   ½   1
        mile

A56
To
Colne

Walk 5: Barrowford

From the Heritage Centre in Barrowford this route follows the course of
Pendle Water and then Blacko Water before climbing through the fields to
Roughlee, the very heart of Pendle Witch country. It returns over
Barrowford Hill to the starting point.

Route: Barrowford – Pendle Water – Water Meetings – Blacko Foot – Roughlee – West Pasture – Pasture Lane – Barrowford.

Start: The Pendle Heritage Centre, Barrowford. Map reference 863398.

Distance: 4 miles (6.5km)

Map: "The South Pennines", number 21 in the O.S. "Outdoor Leisure" series.

Public Transport: There are frequent buses daily (including Sundays) from Colne, Nelson and Burnley. On Summer Sundays and Bank Holidays the Heritage Centre is served by the Pendle Witch Hopper from Burnley, Padiham, Clitheroe and Nelson.

By car: Leave the M65 at Junction 13 and follow the A682 to the Pendle Heritage Centre (signposted). There is a car park on the opposite side of the road.

The Tea Shop

The delightful Tea Room at the Pendle Heritage Centre has the benefit
of extra large windows overlooking the charming and unusual eighteenth century walled gardens. There are tables outside for use in the
warm weather. Although situated in the conservatory with its appropriately green walls, the Tea Room has a modern wooden ceiling with
recessed lighting.

It is run on self-service lines and offers daily specials such as Quiche
Lorraine, Ham Salad and Soup of the Day. There is a variety of sandwiches and jacket potatoes with a wide choice of fillings.

For that touch of afternoon indulgence at the end of the walk you can
choose from a very wide selection of home-made scones, gateaux and
cakes, all served with either cream or ice cream and accompanied by
any number of speciality teas or coffees.

Opening Times: Daily, all year, 10am to 4.30pm. Closed Christmas Day.
Phone: 01282 695366

Pendle Heritage Centre

Pendle Heritage Centre

The Heritage Centre is based in a charming range of stone Grade II Listed Buildings known as Park Hill. It is located by the bridge spanning Pendle Water in the centre of Barrowford. One section is devoted to the history of Park Hill itself from the sixteenth century while another relates the story of Pendle from pre-historic times to the flourishing development of the textile industry during the nineteenth century. There is also a very popular video on the history of the Pendle Witches.

The walled garden has been sympathetically restored and planted only with eighteenth-century flowers. Recently an ancient cruck barn with its "A" frame has been transferred from its original site in Burnley and reconstructed in the grounds of the Heritage Centre.

Apart from the Tea Room there is also a well-stocked Parlour Shop selling herbs, spices, preserves, biscuits and honeys in addition to books of local interest, maps and souvenirs. There is a charge to visit the house, garden and cruck barn but admission to the shop and Tea Room is free.

Opening Times: Daily (including Sundays) from 10am to 4.30pm. Closed Christmas Day. **Phone:** 01282 695366.

The Route

Exit the car park by turning your back to the road and leaving by the stile in the far left-hand corner, the path being signed as part of the

Pendle Way. Pendle Water is on your left with an abundance of wild flowers adorning the banks. Indeed, there are plenty on the small spits of gravel in the middle of the river. To your right is a wire fence and, beyond that, a number of fields. After approximately 300 metres pass to the left of a farm to reach a stile which provides access onto the road, the A682, by the Old Bridge Inn.

Turn left over the bridge and, at the far end, go right into Foreside, a narrow road lined on the left by white weavers' cottages bearing the date 1755 and Brook Dell House with its sundial. Further along a picturesque narrow packhorse bridge with a cobbled surface arches over Pendle Water which now flows on your right.

Admire but do not cross this survival from the past, but rather continue forward as Foreside negotiates a Z bend in front of a partially white-fronted modern house. 10 metres beyond this veer slightly right onto an unsigned tree-lined path alongside Pendle Water. Within 150 metres you are walking through open country where cattle graze the gently sloping valley sides while directly ahead Blacko Hill, with its distinctive tower, gradually comes into view.

Beyond a weir negotiate a small wooden gate by "Old Oak Tree Cottage", a black and white house, and later remain to the right of the boundary fence of a white stone house until reaching a T-junction with a wide track. Turn right over a wooden footbridge and, immediately, go through a squeezer stile on the left onto an unfenced path running along the floor of the valley with Pendle Water on your left once again.

After a further 200 metres the path reaches Waters Meeting, the confluence of Blacko Water with Pendle Water. Stay to the right of Blacko Water to reach a Pendle Way sign after further 100 metres. By this, turn left over a wooden footbridge spanning Blacko Water and, at the far end and by another Pendle Way sign, veer right up the slope while aiming some 60 metres to the right of a five-barred gate where you will meet another Pendle Way sign with a stile adjacent.

Taking your direction from the arm of the sign, cross the centre of the next field to the corner of a wall which marks the highest point of the walk at 179 metres. Beyond this corner the gradient levels and makes for some excellent walking on soft, springy turf while enjoying a distant view of Pendle Hill directly ahead.

Negotiate a stile in the field corner by a footpath sign and maintain the same line of direction to another stile by Blacko Foot Farm. Keep the farm buildings on your right while veering very slightly leftwards for a few metres to a partially obscured stile. Proceed along the narrow path as it squeezes its course between a wall on the right and a fence on the left to reach a wooden gate with footpath signs alongside after 50 metres. This gate provides access to a minor road. However, do not

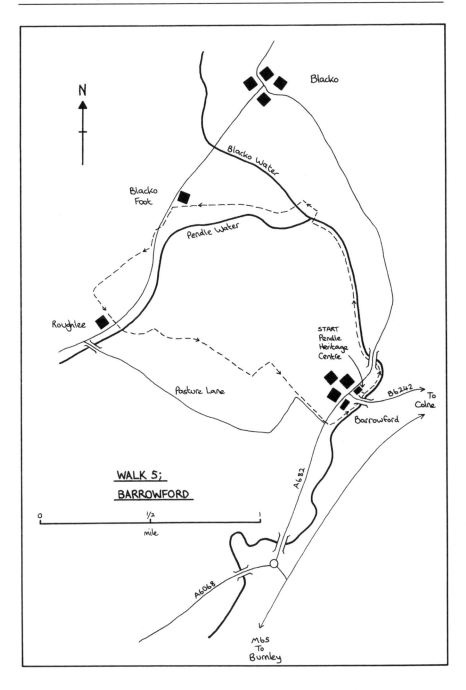

N

Blacko

Blacko Water

Blacko Foot

Pendle Water

Roughlee

START
Pendle
Heritage
Centre

Pasture Lane

B6242
To
Colne

Barrowford

A682

WALK 5;
BARROWFORD

0   ½   1
        mile

A6068

M65
To
Burnley

pass through. Instead, immediately prior to the road, turn left over a stile set into the corner by the small gate to follow a path parallel to the road but which is separated from it by a hedge. After 300 metres turn right over a stile onto the road and turn left, soon reaching a pavement.

Approximately 300 metres after the start of the pavement turn right over another stile complete with a tiny wicket gate which is set between the end of a wall and the start of a hedge. Stay to the left of the wall and then corner the fence on the left before walking to the right of a barn and continuing to the left of the fence while climbing slightly to a squeezer stile with the initials "F.P." painted on it in white.

Follow the same line of direction to the right of some trees and a fence to another stile set into the field corner by a white-painted house which boasts a witch on a broomstick as a weather vane. Remain to the right of the house and then proceed along the drive to a cattle grid and gate. Veer left along the track as it loses height, following the Pendle Way signs until reaching the road running through the hamlet of Roughlee.

For a fine view of Roughlee Hall turn right for 150 metres. Otherwise cross the road directly to a small set of concrete steps, again recognised by a Pendle Way sign. Continue down the slope for 10 metres and use the stepping stones to cross Pendle Water before climbing the slope to another Pendle Way sign.

The path is indistinct in places but veer right up the steep hillside, aiming to pass between two oak trees. Eventually another footpath sign by a wall comes into view to act as your marker. This has a stile alongside. Over that stay to the left of a derelict wall for further excellent field walking with views out to the moors beyond Nelson and Colne.

Pass through the remnants of a hedge and stay forward with the remains of another hedge on your right. The path soon loses height to West Pasture Farm and a ladder stile. Stay forward to the left of a barn and to the right of the farm house to a second stile beyond which the path becomes flanked by hedgerows of rowan, hawthorn, elder and holly.

Emerge from this avenue of trees along a field boundary to a facing fence with a footpath sign some five yards beyond. As there is no means of negotiating the fence at this point, turn left so that the fence is on your right. After 50 metres negotiate a squeezer stile onto a partially surfaced track. Turn right along this, descending for some distance until meeting the road by Pasturegate House and a footpath sign.

Turn left and, using the pavement, walk down Pasture Lane which is lined with old stone houses and cottages. At the T-junction at the bottom of the hill turn left for a few metres and then turn right to cross the A682, continuing forward over the footbridge to enter the park. Turn left and follow the path through the park to the Pendle Heritage Centre.

Walk 6: Downham

The outward stage of this route takes us through gently undulating countryside by the foot of Worsaw Hill before circling round to run along the base of Pendle Hill, finally returning to the village alongside Downham Brook.

Route: Downham – Longlands Wood – Worsaw End – West Lane – Radbrook – Hook Cliffe – Clay House – Downham Brook – Downham.

Start: The car park, Downham village. Map reference 785441.

Distance: 4 miles (6.5km)

Map: "The Forest of Bowland and Ribblesdale", number 41 in the O.S. Outdoor Leisure" series.

Public Transport: There are daily buses from Clitheroe to Downham. On Summer Sundays and Bank Holidays Downham is served by the "Pendle Witch Hopper" from Burnley. Phone: 01200 442226. No Sunday service in winter.

By car: Leave the A59 at map reference 774451 for Chatburn. In the centre of Chatburn village turn left by Hudson's Ice Cream Parlour into Downham Road. Continue for one mile to Downham (signed). The car park and Information Point are at the southern end of the village.

The Tea Shop

There is a cottage atmosphere about the Tea Rooms which are approached through Downham Post Office. The white, papered walls are decorated with paintings of local scenes which are for sale and there is a wonderful collection of tea pots. The tables, with their pink cloths, are arranged to take advantage of the available space.

As well as being the local postmistress, Dianne offers a most tempting collection of home-made cakes ranging from Lemon to Carrot and including Orange and Chocolate. One of the many specialities of the house is Treacle Tart. Her Afternoon and Cream Teas are a real Lancashire delight but for something rather more substantial at lunch-time there is Lasagne, Plate Pie, jacket potatoes and sandwiches of ham, corned beef or genuine Lancashire cheese. Her choice of salads ranges from Norwegian prawns to Lancashire cheese.

Opening Times: April to October: daily 9am to 5pm. Sundays, 11am to 5pm. November to March: daily, including Sundays, 9am to 5pm. (Closed Wednesdays). **Phone:** 01200 441242.

Downham

Dominated by its square-towered church, Downham is a small cluster of limestone houses and cottages clinging to the steep hillside above Downham Brook which, as it gurgles beneath the narrow stone bridge and by the village green, adds to the ambience of this picturesque setting some three miles from Clitheroe. Thanks to the provenance of Lord Clitheroe, who owns Downham, not a single overhead power line, TV aerial, phone wire or yellow parking line disfigures the scene.

Others may challenge Downham's claim to be the prettiest village in Lancashire, but it is difficult to deny its olde-world charm. It achieved some fame as the location for the film "Whistle Down the Wind" starring Hayley Mills.

A church has occupied the site of St Leonard's since at least 1283, although there is some evidence suggesting the existence of one as early as the Norman Conquest and perhaps even earlier than that. The oldest section of the present edifice, the tower, dates from the fifteenth century and, if we believe local tradition, houses three bells transferred from Whalley Abbey at the time of the Dissolution of the Monasteries in the reign of Henry VIII.

The present Squire of Downham is Lord Clitheroe whose family, the

Old house, Downham

Asshetons, have lived in Downham Hall since 1558. The Hall itself, which is not open to the public, was rebuilt in 1835. No village of this type would be complete with its stocks and Downham does not prove to be the exception. The remains are to be seen near the Post Office.

A large stone by the entrance to the Hall is reputed to have marked the graves of two Roman legionaries who died there during a battle with the local tribe, the Brigantes.

The Information Centre, specially designed to blend with the remainder of the village, has won several architectural awards.

Worsaw Hill is composed of limestone and the walls along this section of the route contain many visible examples of fossilised sea creatures.

The Route

By the car park entrance onto West Lane make a sharp right turn onto the lane signed as a public footpath. Proceed between a square stone house on the right and a cottage on the left before reaching a squeezer stile adjacent to a wooden five-barred gate.

Stay alongside the wire fence on your right with the whale-backed hump of Pendle Hill away to your left. At this stage Downham village is still close by.

Where the fence is replaced by a drystone wall another fence comes in from the left to form a narrow grassy passageway for some 50 metres. Where this terminates continue straight ahead, remaining close to the fence on your right and negotiating a wooden five-barred gate to pass Longlands Wood, a small copse on your right which is now home to a small herd of roe deer.

Beyond a squeezer stile in the right-hand corner of the field, stay to the immediate left of another drystone wall. Where this corners away to the right, maintain the same general line of direction over a large field towards a protruding fence with a somewhat crude footpath sign attached.

Having reached it, stay a little to the left of the ensuing fence, as directed, to gain another stone squeezer stile after a distance of some 60 metres. Traverse the bottom of the next field which slopes upwards away to the right to form part of Worsaw End. On the immediate left is an unkempt and overgrown hawthorn hedge.

Where this ends, bend round to the left, losing height for a short distance before passing a stone barn. Ford the very shallow stream and follow the track to reach a stile adjacent to a five-barred gate and a footpath sign pointing to Chatburn at a distance of one mile.

This stile provides access to West Lane. Turn left along the road for approximately 50 metres. By the first footpath sign turn through the squeezer stile on the right. Using the arm of the sign as a guide, cross the field towards the left-hand corner of "Radbrook", a stone house with a carved lintel carrying the initials "T.B.M." and the date of 1690.

Almost immediately before a metal five-barred gate the path forms a junction with another coming in from the left. Turn right along this, pass through the gate and head towards a gap in the facing hedgerow. Follow the clear, well-trodden path through a narrowing field and then continue in the same direction to reach a wide track between "Shepherd's Field", a cottage on your right, and "Hook Cliffe" Farm on your left.

Turn left along the track which clings to the base of the northern flank of Pendle Hill to reach "Hook Cliffe". Follow the track through the farm, first making a left turn between the outbuildings and then a right one to reach two adjacent five-barred gates.

Negotiate the one on the right and stay just to the left of a fence for a short distance to two more five-barred gates, one wooden and the other metal. Pass through the wooden one and DO NOT take the ungated track which runs off at ninety degrees to the left.

Instead, stay with the track which continues to the right of a hedge with Downham Moor rising away to the right. In Spring listen for the bubbling call of the curlew which nests hereabouts. Beyond the next five-barred gate the track narrows into a path. Proceed in the same direction across the centre of a very large field, keeping a decimated row of hawthorns on your right and with Gerna Hill, another limestone knoll, on your left.

From the hawthorns aim for a visible wooden stile in the facing wire fence and then advance just to the right of a stone wall to reach Gerna House.

Pass through a five-barred gate and, keeping the house on your left, maintain direction along the subsequent track to reach Pendle Road by a footpath sign. Turn right for 50 metres but, by the next footpath sign, swing left into the unsurfaced driveway leading to Clay House.

Bear left, with the driveway, to pass between the house on the left and some outbuildings. Corner along the front of Clay House to enter the facing field. There, turn sharply to the left, gradually drawing closer to the hedge on the left whilst heading down the slope. Before reaching the bottom corner of the field maintain a look-out for one of the stone squeezer stiles that are a speciality of the district. It is set fairly inconspicuously into the hedgerow on the left.

Turn left through this and then, immediately, make a right turn along

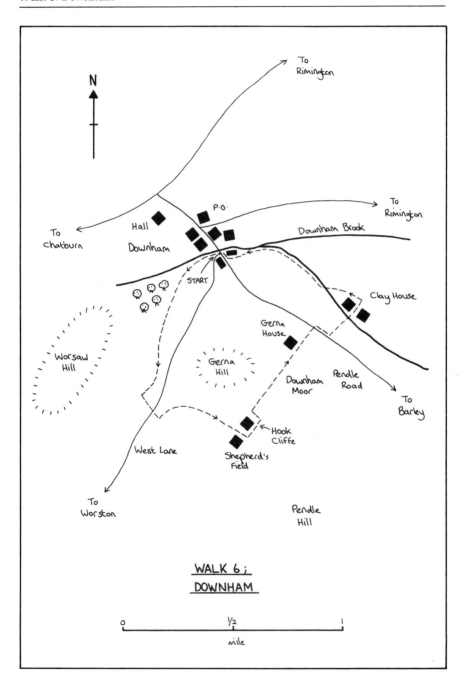

WALK 6;
DOWNHAM

the distinct path which runs along the bank of a stream. Taking care, negotiate a broken footbridge to the opposite bank before following a series of waymarker posts to a recently-repaired stone step stile.

Advance, still with the brook on your right, to a new wooden stile before continuing alongside the stream until it forms its confluence with Downham Brook. Remain with the clear path as it accompanies this through a large meadow until another stone squeezer stile permits access to the village.

Pass the cottages lining both the road and the brook to reach the stone bridge by the village green. For a cup of tea and a sumptuous cream cake, turn right along the main road for the last 200 metres to the Post Office Cafe, observing several interesting buildings on the way.

Hunger and thirst satisfied, return down the hill to the car park.

Walk 7: Barley

Barley is the favourite starting point for the ascent of Pendle Hill.
However, in view of the fact that the upper sections of this path have
suffered severe erosion, this circular walk follows a less frequented route
through Pendle witch country, so avoiding compounding the problems. It
also serves to illustrate that there is a wide variety of walking around this
delightful village.

Route: Barley – Brown House – Pendle House – Under Pendle – Lower Ogden
Reservoir – Barley.

Start: Picnic area and car park, Barley. Map reference 822403.

Distance: 3 miles (4.8km)

Map: "The Forest of Bowland and Ribblesdale", number 41 in the O.S.
"Outdoor Leisure" series.

Public Transport: Buses from Clitheroe, Nelson and Burnley on certain weekdays. On
Summer Sundays and Bank Holidays Barley is served by the "Pendle
Witch Hopper" from Burnley, Clitheroe and Nelson. Phone: 01200
442226 for details.

By car: Leave the A59, Preston to Skipton trunk road, at map reference 768432
and follow the road signed for Chatburn and Downham. From
Downham take the unclassified but signposted road to Barley. From
the A6068 in Fence, follow the signs to Newchurch and Barley along
narrow, unclassified roads.

The Tea Shop

The Barley Tea Room is housed in what was once the front room of a
seventeenth century handloom weaver's cottage, its antiquity only too
evident from the beamed ceiling. When the nearby reservoirs were
constructed during the nineteenth century it served as a bakery to keep
the workmen fed.

The white walls are adorned with a variety of countryside pictures
while the pine tables are matched by either stools, chairs or benches.
The present owners, Mike and Lorraine Goldsborough, have been
serving meals here for seven years.

The walkers' favourite is the "Broth and Dumpling", a speciality of
the house, followed, perhaps, by a large Farmhouse Fruit Scone or

Appley Dappley Cake served warm with cream. Lorraine makes a delightful Coffee and Walnut Cake in addition to Pavlova and a variety of fruit pies dependent on the season.

There is the usual selection of sandwiches and jacket potatoes but, for the really hungry, there is a devilishly tempting dish of Dales Pork Sausages with onion rings. If that does not appeal, then the pie of the day is always worthwhile. Tea and coffee flow in abundance. **Opening Times:** Summer: daily 12am to 5pm. (5.30pm on Sundays). Winter: Saturdays and Sundays only, 12.am to 5pm. **Phone:** 01282 694127.

Barley

Barley is an attractive village of stone-built cottages nestling beneath the formidable hulk of Pendle, perhaps the county's most famous hill. Seven miles (11km) in length and rising to 557 metres (almost 2,000 feet), it forms a familiar landmark for miles around. When the Spanish Armada approached in 1588 the warning beacon on its summit was one of a string that stretched from Cornwall to the Scottish Borders.

During the early seventeenth century it formed the spectacular backdrop to the grim tales of the Lancashire Witches, some of whom are closely associated with the ancient farmhouses along this route.

In 1653 George Fox climbed to the summit where he is reputed to have received his Divine inspiration for the formation of the Society of Friends. Subsequently, the Quakers enjoyed a strong following in the Pendle and Bowland areas.

Barley from the lower slopes of Pendle Hill

The Route

In the car park take the path alongside the Information Centre, following it through the picnic area until it emerges onto Clitheroe Road, the main thoroughfare through the village of Barley.

Turn right, walking through the village and passing the Pendle Hotel on your left and the Tea Room on your right. Opposite the Methodist Church and by a footpath sign, turn left along a stretch of the Pendle Way with a brook flowing on your right.

After 150 metres and beyond the first stile, the path enters open country with the formidable brooding mass of Pendle Hill ahead. After crossing a wooden footbridge the path curves round to the left, still following the course of the stream, to reach a wall corner. A red notice indicates that the path crosses a bridge so veer right to cross another footbridge before meeting a narrow, metalled road.

Turn left. A few metres before the Mirewater Trout Fishery pass a white house on your right and, some 10 metres beyond, make a right turn through a metal kissing gate accompanied by both a public footpath sign and a Pendle Way sign.

The path, which travels between two fences, climbs and crosses a footbridge on its way to reach a waymarked stile. Continue upwards, now to the left of a fence with foxgloves, red campion, ragged robin and buttercups lining the route.

Eventually the path passes through a kissing gate by Brown House. Stay to the right of the house, following the signs to Pendle, as the route climbs towards the wall on the right where there is another stile and another sign.

Over the stile turn left and walk to the right of a wall until, approximately 25 metres before a facing wall, veer right across the field to a small wooden gate in the field corner.

Pass through and continue up the subsequent field a shade to the left of a wall while directing your steps towards the left-hand corner of Pendle House.

Negotiate a stile alongside the house and, ignoring all the signs to Pendle, make a left turn to tread an indistinct path immediately to the right of a wall. After a few yards the path becomes much clearer and, after 150 metres, passes through a derelict gateway before pursuing its course through a scattering of reeds.

The steep slopes of Pendle are on the immediate right while, in the distance to your left, are several reservoirs. Each footstep flushes meadow pipits and skylarks from the heather and rough grassland. The path clings to the contour, staying well above the wall on the left.

After a considerable distance a stile, adjacent to a metal five-barred gate, is reached. Over that turn diagonally left down the slope to a ladder stile.

Having negotiated that, walk between the now-derelict Under Pendle House on your left and a new house on the right before passing to the left of a white house and then negotiating a wooden five-barred gate onto a walled lane.

Beyond a second five-barred gate the lane becomes fenced. Stay along the lane by some barns and sheep pens before passing through a double five-barred gate for a slight climb as the lane curves round to the right.

At the top of the climb the lane bends right, and then left, before reaching a junction. The track you have just used is signed to Under Pendle, another track is leads to Ogden Hill. Ignore both. Stay forward to pass through a gateway and immediately make an acute turn to the left onto a field path heading towards a plantation.

Gradually veer towards the right, away from the wall towards a wooden stile. Over this advance to a second stile after 2 metres and then remain forward through the plantation on a very distinct path while losing altitude all the time.

On gaining another stile make a left turn along the chatter track which follows the northern bank of Lower Ogden Reservoir. Beyond the embankment wall the track acquires a surface and soon descends towards Barley where it emerges directly opposite the car park and picnic site.

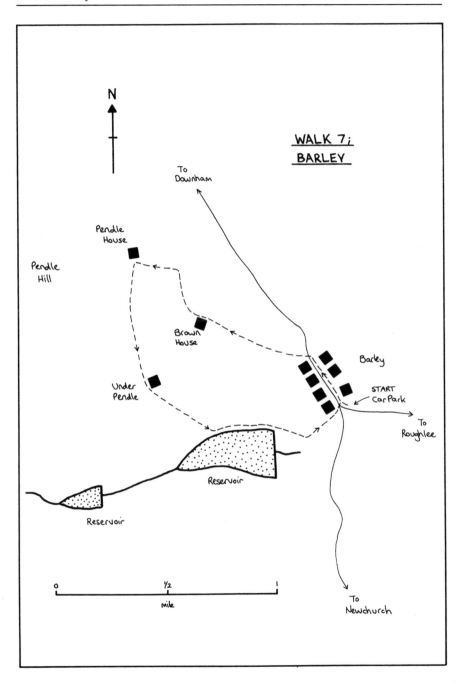

N

To
Downham

WALK 7;
BARLEY

Pendle
House

Pendle
Hill

Brown
House

Barley

Under
Pendle

START
Car Park

To
Roughlee

Reservoir

Reservoir

To
Newchurch

0   ½   1
        mile

Walk 8: Clitheroe

An easy, level route through a lush pastoral landscape using field and riverside paths with views of the nearby fells.

Route: Clitheroe – Waddow Hall – Brungerley Bridge – Hill Top – West Bradford Bridge – Brungerley Park – Clitheroe

Start: Chester Avenue car park, Clitheroe. Map reference 742422.

Distance: 4¼ miles (7km)

Map: "The Forest of Bowland and Ribblesdale", number 41 in the O.S. "Outdoor Leisure" series.

Public Transport: Rail: Clitheroe is served by an hourly train service from Manchester Victoria, Salford, Bolton and Blackburn from Mondays to Saturdays. By changing at either Salford Crescent or Bolton it is possible to travel from Manchester Piccadilly or Manchester Airport. There is a reduced service on Summer Sundays. Also on Summer Sundays there are trains from Blackpool and Preston as part of the Dales Rail Service. **Phone:** 01200 443800 or 0161 832 8353.
Bus: Clitheroe is served by frequent daily buses (including Sundays) from Manchester, Southport, Preston, Blackburn, Darwen, Bolton, Bury and Skipton. Buses from Longridge and Settle, daily (except Sundays.).

By car: Clitheroe lies on the A671 which is signed from the A59, Preston to Skipton road. There is ample free parking.

The Tea Shop

The sheer elegance of the Apricot Meringue disguises the lurking temptations. Its Afternoon Teas and Cream Teas have few peers. The sandwiches are perfect while the scones, served with liberal helpings of cream and preserves, melt in the mouth. The vast array of home-made cakes and gateaux create difficult problems of choice but, whatever the decision, nothing will go wrong. Frangipane Custard Tarts, Passion Cake, Carrot and Walnut Cake and Lemon Meringue are but four of the mouth-watering varieties on offer. Waffles, served with cream or ice cream and topped with strawberries, pineapple, black cherries and maple syrup are a speciality of the house.

For anyone in search of fare more substantial there is an amazing list of open and closed sandwiches, all served with a gargantuan salad, jacket potatoes, soup, bacon chops with two fried eggs, Ploughman's Platter, Steak and Kidney Pie, Cottage Pie or Cheese Bites. Vegetarians can regale themselves with 'Red Dragon Pie'. To accompany any of these dishes there is a selection of speciality teas, coffees and soft drinks.

The white wrought-iron tables with their pink tablecloths and matching chairs blend perfectly with the decor which again is pink but contrasted by a darker floral wall paper and a classical plaster frieze. When the weather is clement there is the Rose Tea Garden. The Apricot Meringue stands in Clitheroe's King Street, close to the railway station and the car park from which this walk starts.

Opening Times: Monday to Saturday: 9am to 5pm. (4pm on Wednesdays). Closed on Sundays. **Phone:** 01200 26933.

Clitheroe

Dominated by the square stone keep of its castle, Clitheroe is an ancient market town commanding a strategic position in the Ribble Valley, overlooked by slopes of Pendle Hill while, at the same time, guarding the entrance to the Forest of Bowland. The castle dates from 1186 when it was constructed by Robert de Lacy to protect his extensive estates in the area. The keep is reckoned to be the smallest of any castle in England with rooms only 20 feet square. The top of the castle is reached by a spiral stone staircase.

It last saw action in 1644 when, after being held by Royalist soldiers for several weeks, it was captured by the Roundheads and more or less razed to the ground. The keep was restored in 1848 and today houses a museum of local history which is well worth visiting.

Clitheroe remains a pleasant if small bustling town with many individual shops including Cowman's Sausage Shop which advertises no fewer than 47 varieties including pork, venison, leek and wild boar. Equally interesting is Byrne's, the wine merchants, with a cellar of more than 100 malt whiskies. Clitheroe Market, one of the best in Lancashire, is held on Tuesdays and Saturdays.

Waddow Hall

Waddow Hall was built and owned by the Garnett family who operated a large mill a little further downstream. The weir at the spot where the footpath meets the river bank is a noted local viewpoint for watching the salmon leap as they swim up the Ribble for the spawning season.

Visible on the far bank, in front of the hall, is a well which has a rather gruesome legend attached to it. At some unspecified date Peg O'Nell, a servant girl, became involved in an argument with her mistress over the carrying of water from this well. As Peg departed on her errand, her employer cried out, "I hope you fall and break your neck."

As in all such stories the inevitable happened and now there is a headless statue of the kneeling girl near the river bank. Her troubled spirit is alleged to haunt the hall but the present owners, the Girl Guides' Association, deny this. It is now used as a Commonwealth Training Centre.

The Route

Exit the Chester Avenue car park by turning right and, almost at once, making a left turn under the railway bridge. At the far end of this turn right and walk by the railway station on your right and continue beyond the market which is on your left. At the far end of this road make another right turn, this time into Wesleyan Row.

Continue over the railway bridge but, at the far end, turn into Castle View which has modern bungalows on the right and solid stone terraced housing on the left. Follow this road round to the left as it changes its name to Kirkmoor Road.

A few metres beyond where the houses end, and the road bends through ninety degrees to the left to become "Back Commons", turn right over a wooden stile by a wooden five-barred gate.

This path, obviously well patronised, strikes out diagonally left to a stile in a hawthorn hedge before maintaining direction across a small field to a wooden kissing gate. Through this make a left turn as the path runs close by a line of trees on your right. Stay with this boundary to a second kissing gate to be found in the right-hand corner of the field. Then, veer to the right, heading towards the large, cream-coloured house that is Waddow Hall although it stands on the far bank of the Ribble.

On reaching a hawthorn hedge above the weir in the river swing to the right, with the path, as it descends a flight of steps to gain the river bank. At the foot of the steps maintain direction eastwards along the river bank with the river on your left and Waddow Hall clearly visible on the far side. Pass through a kissing gate and over a stone-slabbed footbridge while heading towards Brungerley Bridge. Boy Bank Wood clothes the steep slopes on your right.

Almost immediately before the bridge turn right over a substantial wooden footbridge to reach a flight of stone steps topped by a step stile which provides an exit onto Waddington Road.

Exercising extreme caution in the absence of any pavements, turn left over the bridge. Some 50 metres beyond and by a footpath sign

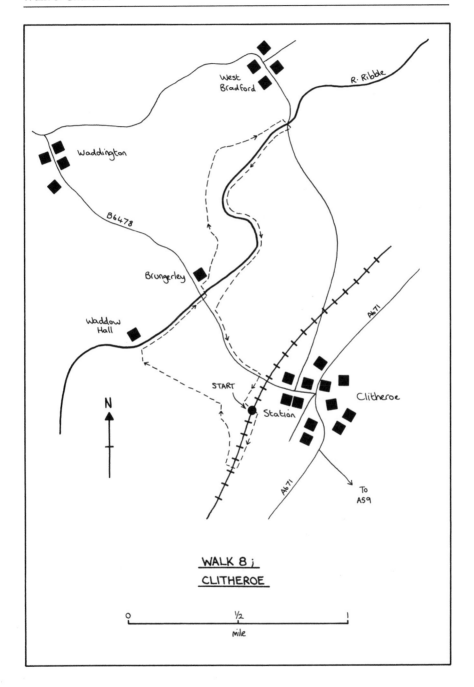

West
Bradford

R. Ribble

Waddington

B6478

Brungerley

Waddow
Hall

A671

START

N

Station

Clitheroe

A671

To
A59

WALK 8 ;
CLITHEROE

0   ½   1
mile

West Bradford bridge

indicating a path to West Bradford, veer right through a metal kissing gate housed in a wooden frame which is alongside a metal five-barred gate.

The broad track climbs slightly to pass to the right of Brungerley Farm. This section of the route may be extremely muddy after wet weather. Beyond the farm the track continues upwards between tall hawthorn hedges until emerging into open country by Hill Top. Immediately, by a fence corner, turn left through ninety degrees, ignoring a narrower path which continues directly ahead.

The field boundary is on your left while, in the far distance is a splendid view of Newton Fell and some of the other landmarks of Bowland. On reaching the left-hand corner of the field pass through a metal five-barred gate before veering slightly right to a concrete footbridge.

Fifty yards beyond this turn right over a wooden stile before going slightly left to cross a second concrete footbridge set into a gateless gateway. Maintain your general direction across the next field to a stile which is followed, within a few yards, by a single flag footbridge. Continue forwards, a distance of some 20 metres to the left of a boundary fence, to a stile and then proceed straight ahead to another stile.

However, do not negotiate this. Instead, immediately before it, turn right to reach a stile after 10 metres. Then advance for 15 metres on the clear path through some hawthorn trees to yet another stile which is waymarked.

Beyond this gradually move leftwards, as directed, heading for the gap between a hedge on the left and a short stretch of stone wall on the right. Ahead, only a short distance away, is West Bradford Bridge and all the time the distinct path draws closer to the northern bank of the Ribble.

On reaching the left end of West Bradford Bridge negotiate the stile and ascend another flight of stone steps to emerge onto the road leading into West Bradford village.

Turn right over the bridge to reach a footpath sign. By this turn right down a flight of three steps onto the well-used path which clings closely to the southern bank of the Ribble and forms part of the Ribble Way, another long distance walking route from the estuary into the Yorkshire Dales.

Negotiate a stone step stile which is almost adjacent to a dilapidated wooden five-barred gate and then proceed to a wooden stile. Remain along the riverside path as it arcs round in a great sweep to the left to another stile followed after a short distance by yet another. At this point, while the river bends away to the right, the stile affords an entry into the woodlands of Brungerley Park.

The path climbs fairly steeply for a few metres to a T-junction where a right turn is made onto a broad path which maintains a level course with the Ribble down below on the right. At one point you will pass a piece of carved wooden sculpture in the form of an orientation station showing the different points of the compass.

Ignoring all side paths, stay with the main route until it curves slightly left to a Y-junction. Fork right to reach the main gates to the park and Waddington Road.

Turn left along this passing residential property and a couple of cemeteries, one on either side of the road. A short distance before reaching the railway bridge turn right into Chester Avenue to reach the car park from which you started.

Walk 9: Whalley

A short walk using field paths and country lanes to climb Whalley Nab for the breathtaking view along the Ribble Valley and of Pendle Hill.

Route: Whalley Abbey – Nab Wood – Whalley Banks – Heys Farm – Berry Lane – Shawcliff Lane – Billington – Whalley Abbey.

Start: Whalley Abbey, Whalley. Map reference 731361.

Distance: 3½ miles (5.5km)

Map: "Longridge and Great Harwood", number 680 in the O.S. "Pathfinder" series.

Public Transport: Rail: Whalley is served by frequent daily trains from Clitheroe, Manchester Victoria, Bolton and Blackburn. On Summer Sundays and Bank Holidays there is a restricted service but additional trains from Blackpool, Preston and Blackburn as part of the Dales Rail service. **Bus:** There are frequent daily buses (including Sundays) from Clitheroe, Blackburn, Bolton, Manchester, Darwen, Accrington, Bury, Preston, Southport and Skipton.

By car: Whalley is approximately 3 miles from Clitheroe and is signed from the A59 Preston to Skipton road. It is also signed from the Padiham to Clitheroe road. There is ample car parking.

The Tea Shop

As the name suggests, the Cloisters Coffee Shop is located within the former cloisters of the Cistercian Abbey. Its high roof is heavily beamed while the walls are of the original stonework. The great vaulted arches have been glazed.

It operates a counter service but has a wide menu including baked potatoes with various fillings, sandwiches with salad garnish, light snacks such as Creamed Mushrooms, salads and Afternoon Teas consisting of a pot of tea, sandwiches of choice, scone with cream and preserve and a home-made cake. There is All-Butter Shortbread, Sticky Parkin, Flapjacks and Fruit Cake, just to mention a few. The Cloisters offers a choice of coffees and speciality teas along with various cold beverages and soft drinks.

Opening Hours: Daily all year, 11am to 5pm. Closed Christmas Day. **Phone:** 01254 822268

Whalley

The Cistercian Abbey of Whalley was established in 1296, the last religious foundation in Lancashire, although the actual community had previously been located at Stanlow in Cheshire from 1172. With the Pope's permission, they transferred to lands which they owned already.

Some idea of its enormous size may be gained from the fact that although the foundation stone of the Abbey Church was laid in 1330, the first Mass was not celebrated there until 1380. Little now remains of the cathedral-like church except the foundations. The canopied stalls survive in the nearby parish church of St Mary and All Angels.

Considerable portions of the monks' dormitory, the cloisters and a storehouse built in 1415 are well preserved. The Abbot's House (not open to visitors) was rebuilt as a Tudor manor house by Richard Assheton and is now used as a Conference Centre by the Anglican Diocese of Blackburn.

The parish church pre-dates the Abbey by a century and there is evidence of an even earlier Christian settlement in the form of three pre-Conquest stone crosses in the churchyard. The interior roof displays some of the finest woodwork in Lancashire and this is matched by the seventeenth century pews and the choir stalls which were transferred from the Abbey at the time of the Reformation.

Whalley Abbey

The small town of Whalley is filled with fascinating shops and old houses, a mixture of Tudor and Georgian, particularly around the Square. Its antiquity is illustrated by some of the medieval stonework to be found in the bridge spanning the River Calder. It was this position as a river crossing which elevated Whalley into a place of considerable importance for several centuries. Equally impressive is the red brick viaduct which now carries the railway across the valley.

The Route

From the Abbey grounds walk towards the Square with its ancient houses and pass the parish church to enter Church Lane. This leads to the main road through the town. Turn right along this but, at the junction by "The Swan", stay forward into King Street.

Cross the River Calder but, at the far end of the bridge, fork left into Moor Lane. After 100 metres and by a bridleway sign, make another left fork into a narrow lane which climbs steeply with a wall on your left and a bank on the right. It is lined with bramble and red campion in summer and is the haunt of robins, wrens and blackbirds.

After a further 200 metres, and by a seat, go left, the path coursing its way just inside a wire fence with a splendid view over the River Calder to Whalley and Longridge Fell. The path continues its upward ascent but, after a short flight of three ancient stone steps, it swings round to the left inside the boundary of Nab Wood. From that point onwards the steep gradient eases.

Eventually the path forms a junction with wide track. Turn left along this, soon passing a fine-looking house, "Three Views". Continue through a wooden gate onto a much narrower, tree-lined path which makes its way along the contour before widening and acquiring a metalled surface by Fielden Farm.

Stay forward to pass Whalley Banks Farm on the left before reaching an old white stone farmhouse. Here the lane bends to the right. Leave it at this juncture to maintain direction along a narrower path which is signed to Great Harwood.

After 100 metres, and in front of a wooden five-barred gate, veer leftwards as directed by the yellow arrow on the tree. Lose a little height to a stile and then continue down the grassy slope to reach a T-junction in the path network after 50 metres. Turn right, pass through a metal five-barred gate and turn sharp left along the wide lane. Eventually this leads to a junction with Berry's Lane by Heys Farm. Turn right for the steep climb up Berry's Lane for approximately 1km to reach another T-junction, this time by "Moor-End", a white wooden house which stands on the corner.

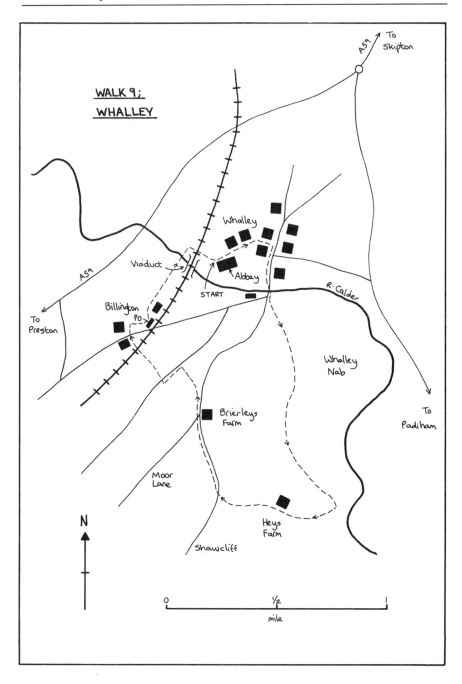

WALK 9;
WHALLEY

To
Skipton
A59

Whalley

Viaduct

A59

Abbey

R. Calder

START

To
Preston

Billington
PO

Whalley
Nab

To
Padiham

Brierleys
Farm

Moor
Lane

N

Heys
Farm

Shawcliff

0   ½   1
            mile

Turn right into Shawcliff Lane, following it until it forms an inverted Y-junction with Moor Lane just below a television transmitter mast. Maintain the same line of direction along Moor Lane for approximately 100 metres to a footpath sign. Turn left over the adjacent stile before veering slightly towards the right through the trees on a clear path to reach another stile after 200 metres.

Proceed in the same direction a little to the left of a fence. The sloping grassy terrace creates ideal walking conditions as its drops steeply to a squeezer stile alongside a footpath sign on Whalley Old Road.

Turn left along this, pass a row of stone cottages on your right and, after 100 metres and by another footpath sign, make a right turn through a wooden kissing gate. Stay close to the hedge on your right until, in the bottom corner of the field, you negotiate a small, wooden gate. Stop, look and listen before crossing the railway lines to a second gate and then staying forward between the houses for a few yards to meet Calder Avenue. Turn right along this to meet a main road after 75 metres.

Turn right once more and, just beyond the Post Office and immediately before the railway bridge, turn left as directed by the footpath sign. Negotiate a stile after 10 metres and a second after a further 20 metres. Cross a small field to a third stile and then advance by some corrugated sheeting on your left to a fourth stile.

Over that turn sharply to the right. After about 150 metres and by the corner of some allotments, negotiate a kissing gate to traverse another small field to a second kissing gate. Once again turn right for a few metres to reach Longworth Road.

Cross directly to a footpath sign which stands by arch number four of the Whalley railway viaduct. Follow the path which runs alongside the towering viaduct and crosses the River Calder by the splendid metal footbridge known as "Old Sol's". The present fine structure is a replacement for the one originally donated by Solomon Longworth, the then owner of Judge Walmsley's Mill.

On emerging onto a narrow road turn right, pass beneath the arch of the Abbey gatehouse, and stay forward until reaching the main entrance to the Abbey.

Walk 10: Great Mitton

Using mainly field paths but including two very short lengths of road, this route follows the course of the Ribble before returning over rich pastureland.

Route: Eddisford Bridge – Siddows – Fishes and Peggy Hill – Great Mitton – Malkin Lane – Brick House – Eddisford Bridge.

Start: Free car park by Eddisford Bridge, near Clitheroe. Map reference 726414.

Distance: 6 miles (9.6km)

Map: "The Forest of Bowland and Ribblesdale", number 41 in the O.S. "Outdoor Leisure" series.

Public Transport: Rail: Clitheroe is served by an hourly train service from Manchester Victoria, Salford, Bolton and Blackburn from Mondays to Saturdays. By changing at either Salford Crescent or Bolton it is possible to travel from Manchester Piccadilly or Manchester Airport. There is a reduced service on Summer Sundays. Also on Summer Sundays there are trains from Blackpool and Preston as part of the Dales Rail service. **Phone:** 01200 443800 or 0161 832 8353.
Buses: Clitheroe is served by frequent daily buses (including Sundays) from Manchester, Southport, Preston, Blackburn, Darwen, Bolton, Bury and Skipton. Buses from Longridge and Settle daily, except Sundays. Either walk the one mile from Clitheroe railway station or use the Clitheroe to Longridge or the Clitheroe to Chipping bus service (not Sundays) and alight at Eddisford Bridge.

By car: Clitheroe lies on the A671 which is signed from the A59, Preston to Skipton road. From the centre of Clitheroe follow the B6246 Clitheroe to Whalley road. Alternatively, it is possible to leave the A59 for Whalley and follow the B6246 to Eddisford Bridge. The car park near Eddisford Bridge is free.

The Tea Shop

The Hillcrest Tea Rooms stand, appropriately on the crest of the hill as the road climbs up from Mitton Bridge towards Clitheroe. Housed in a former blacksmith's workshop, they are all wooden beams and exposed stonework. The plain walls are decorated with dried flower arrangements and there is piped classical music to accompany your meal. For those warm, sunny afternoons there are tables in the large garden which supplies the gooseberries, apples and plums used in the fruit pies.

Run by Anne Beardsworth, who is renowned for her cooking, the menu is a very tempting invitation to suit all appetites.

Specialities of the house include Lemon Sole stuffed with Crab Meat, Plate Meat Pie, Mushrooms in Garlic Butter and Spinach and Mushroom Lasagne.

There is a mouth-watering and devilish array of sweets which few will have the will power to resist. It includes Sticky Toffee Pudding, Rhubarb Crumble, Sherry Trifle and Summer Pudding, not to mention a seemingly endless list of freshly- baked gateaux and cakes. All are accompanied by a selection of speciality teas, coffees and soft drinks.

Opening Times: Monday to Saturday, all year, 10am to 5pm. Sunday, all year, 10am to 6pm. **Phone:** 01254 826573.

St Oswald's Church

The name "Mitton" is derived from the Saxon "Mythe" which, apparently, meant "a farmstead at the meeting of two rivers", the two rivers in question being the Ribble and the Hodder. In early Christian times the parish was extremely extensive embracing such distant villages as Waddington, West Bradford and Aighton.

It merited a mention in the Domesday Book of 1086 and the first record of the church dates from 1103 when a certain gentleman by the name of Ralph was the vicar. His name and all those of his successors are listed on a board inside the church, the current incumbent being John Birbeck, appointed in 1992.

In those very early days the church may have been a wooden building of Saxon origin but the present edifice dates from 1270 when the nave was built in the Early English style. This was followed in quick succession by the chancel, the sedilia, piscina and south porch. It is of somewhat unusual construction in that admission is gained by descending a flight of four steps inside the door. The pews are Jacobean while the pulpit is believed to date from the reign of Queen Anne, 1702 to 1714.

One of the glories of this church is the beautifully carved chancel screen which was transferred from Sawley Abbey at the time of the Dissolution of the Monasteries in the reign of Henry VIII. Another of its many attractions is the Shireburne Chapel where several members of this distinguished family are buried.

The Route

Although there are one or two off-road parking spaces in Great Mitton, Eddisford Bridge was chosen as the starting point for this walk because it enjoys the advantage of a very large and free car park.

From the car park entrance turn left along the B6243, using the segregated footpath to pass the entrance to the caravan park on your left while descending towards Eddisford Bridge which spans the River Ribble.

Immediately before the bridge, and by a Ribble Way Information Panel, turn left along the riverside path to walk behind a long row of seats whilst passing through the picnic area. The good distinct path very soon passes between the river on your right and a fence on your left to reach a wooden kissing gate bearing the Ribble Way legend.

Turn left through this gate and then turn right, maintaining the same direction but climbing gently towards some trees and a second way-marked kissing gate. Through this swing leftwards, as directed by the waymark, to cross a field diagonally to meet another kissing gate in the opposite corner.

Having negotiated this turn right for a distance of 10 metres to meet a T-junction of lanes.

Turn left, as suggested by another Ribble Way sign, to a second T-junction, this time with Henthorn Road. Ignore the facing stile and make yet another right turn, first crossing a small stone bridge and then passing Siddows Farm which is on your right. Keep Mill House on your left and also the Waste Disposal Site before proceeding along the narrow, surfaced lane until meeting the Ribble again on your right.

Continue through a gateway bearing the sign, "Private Road: Footpath Only". Continue in the same direction to pass the uniquely-named "Fishes and Peggy Hill" Farm on your left and, just beyond, a house on your right. On reaching a large facing cattle shed at Shuttleworth Farm make a right turn and then a left one to walk alongside the building. Stay forward along a wide track with the Ribble to your right as it flows through lush, riverside meadows with herons hunting its waters.

Pass an aqueduct carrying several large pipes over the river and, shortly afterwards, a small weir where, in season, salmon may be seen leaping as they make their way upstream to their spawning grounds.

By a small brick building, turn left through forty five degrees, as instructed by a footpath sign, so moving away from the Ribble and obtaining your first glimpse of Great Mitton church in the far distance.

Cross a concrete footbridge over Barrow Brook to climb slightly for approximately 50 metres to a kissing gate. Stay forward to the left of a fence along the field boundary, as the path continues upwards to a

Great Mitton Church

wooden stile set into a short stretch of facing fence. Continue to the left of a fence, following it round the boundary of a large field while descending to another stile alongside a metal five-barred gate which provides access to the B6246.

Turn right along the road to pass the Aspinall Arms and, almost immediately, to cross the sloping Mitton Bridge before climbing with the road to the Hillcrest Tea Rooms.

By the far corner of the café turn sharp right away from the B6246 and into a minor road. Pass the stone-built medieval church of All Hallows, the "Old Vicarage" and "The Barn" as the narrow road curves round sharply to the left.

Opposite a stone house on the left look for a footpath sign. By this make a right turn into Malkin Lane, a name redolent of the Lancashire Witches. It passes between overgrown hedgerows and is lined with stinging nettles. Negotiate a stile to continue along the grassy bridleway with Waddington Fell and Pendle Hill both visible, albeit some distance away.

After a second stile by a long, low and white shed, continue forwards while maintaining a sharp eye open for a rusty metal five-barred gate in the hedgerow on the left. Do not be tempted to continue further along

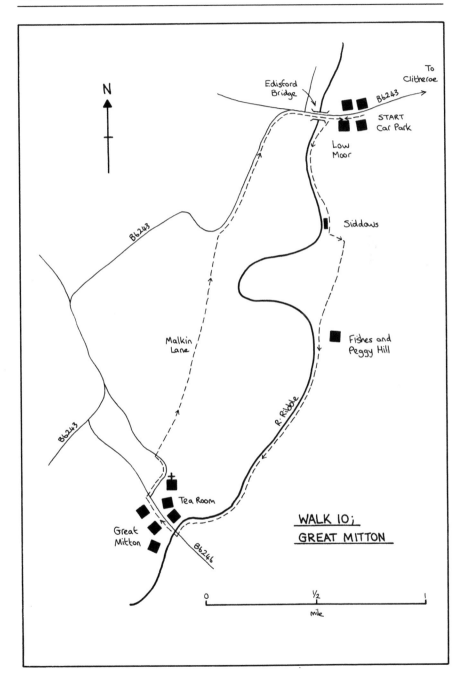

N

To Clitheroe

Edisford Bridge

B6243

START Car Park

Low Moor

B6243

Siddows

Malkin Lane

Fishes and Peggy Hill

R. Ribble

B6243

Tea Room

Great Mitton

B6246

WALK 10;
GREAT MITTON

0   ½   1
         mile

the lane because you will eventually find all further progress obstructed. Instead, at this point, turn left over the stile adjacent to the gate and turn right at once, so maintaining the same general direction but now to the left of a hedge.

The indistinct path leads to a stile some 50 metres to the left of the field corner. Over this proceed for 10 metres and then make a left turn over a footbridge and, at the far end, turn right, thereby continuing in your original direction. Remain to the left of a stream as it rounds an area of scrub, eventually reaching another stile adjacent to a metal five-barred gate in the right-hand corner of the field.

Over the stile turn right to be faced with a choice of two waymarks, one pointing forward and another to the left. Take the one to the left and negotiate a metal five-barred gate which permits passage to a wide chatter track. Follow this until meeting the B6246 by Brick House Barn, surprisingly a stone building now converted into a house.

Turn right, using the wide grass verge to follow the road back across Eddisford Bridge to the starting point.

Walk 11: Hurst Green

One of the most delightful walks in rural Lancashire, this route starts from an attractive village of stone houses to follow the river bank before climbing to cross the parkland surrounding one of the country's leading public schools.

Route: Hurst Green – Ribble Way – Jumbles – Fox Fields Farm – Stonyhurst College – Hurst Green.

Start: The Shireburn Arms Hotel, Hurst Green. Map reference 685378.

Distance: 4 miles (6.5km)

Map: "Great Harwood and Longridge", number 680 in the O.S. "Pathfinder" series.

Public Transport: Hurst Green is served by bus service number 105 from Clitheroe, Longridge and Chipping. Several buses daily, including Saturday. No Sunday service. Phone 01282 425144 for detailed times. The Hodder Valley Rambler, service number 44 from Blackpool and Preston, calls at Hurst Green on Summer Sundays. Leaflets from the Tourist Information centre, Clitheroe. Phone 01200 442226 or Blackpool 01253 751485 or Preston 01772 556618.

By car: Hurst Green is located on the B6243 Clitheroe to Longridge road. It may also be approached by leaving the A59 Preston to Skipton road at Copster Green (map reference 671335) and following the signs to Ribchester. After crossing the Ribble by Ribchester Bridge and entering the village of Dutton, make a right turn into Gallows Lane which is signed to Hurst Green. There is no official car park but there are several places in the village where roadside parking is possible. There is a car park in front of the Village Hall but this should only be used when the Hall is not in use.

The Tea Shop

There are no net curtains or chintzy covers in the Tea Rooms which form part of the Shireburn Arms Hotel. This occupies a prominent position in the centre of Hurst Green village. With its flagged stone floor, thick stone walls painted white and small-paned windows, the café has a reassuringly northern, indeed Lancastrian, atmosphere.

This does not mean, however, that the Tea Rooms are spartan. On the contrary they exude a warmth and cosiness that is more than welcome after a long walk. The chairs are plush and the tables are covered with green check tablecloths. The white walls are not over-decorated but display a few items of brassware and, appropriately for witch country, several besom brooms.

A notice outside announces, "Walkers Welcome". This is not an idle boast for the friendliness and service offered by the staff only serves to emphasise all that has ever been written about the legendary Lancashire hospitality. Nothing, it would appear, is too much trouble.

The fare offered is simple and wholesome. There is Soup of the Day, sandwiches both hot and cold with various fillings, salads and a fine selection of home-baked cakes. Beverages include a selection of teas, including herbal, hot chocolate, coffee and Horlicks.

Opening Times: 10am to 5pm daily, all year. **Phone:** 01254 826518.

Stonyhurst

Stonyhurst College offers the most outstanding view in the entire Ribble Valley and it is a view which compares favourably with most others in England. It is best appreciated by approaching from Hurst Green.

The driveway begins on the edge of the village, climbs gently between woodlands and, by the statue of Our Lady, turns right through ninety degrees to cross open parkland and pass between two ornamental lakes to the impressive frontage. The archway of the main entrance is flanked by four tiers of classical columns and topped by octagonal turrets with their domes and eagles.

Today it is a famous Catholic public school but it began as an ordinary country residence. The estate was presented to Walter Bayley by King Edward I but, when Richard Bayley married a daughter of Sir Richard Shireburn in 1377, he assumed his wife's surname and so began the close association between that family and Stonyhurst that was to endure for four hundred years.

During the early years of the sixteenth century Hugh Shireburn made considerable additions to the house but it was Sir Richard Shireburn, who inherited the property in 1537 who was responsible for the re-building on a grand scale. Late in the following century Sir Nicholas added the eagle towers and was also instrumental in creating a new layout for the grounds. It was during his lifetime that the two ornamen-tal lakes were constructed according to the designs of James 11@s gardener, Henry Wise.

Oliver Cromwell stayed at Stonyhurst on the eve of the Battle of Preston during the Civil War but, as this was a staunch Catholic

Almshouses at Hurst Green

household, he is said to have been afraid of assassination. To reduce the risk of a premature death he slept on the table in the middle of the room with his sword and pistol close at hand.

During the eighteenth century the Shireburn line came to an end and the estate passed to the Weld family who were also Catholic. When the French Revolution broke out in 1789 the Jesuit Order was compelled to close its school at St Omer in northern France. So Thomas Weld, who had been a pupil at the school, offered Stonyhurst as a sanctuary. Ever since the Jesuits and Stonyhurst have been linked and today it is one of the foremost public school in the country. Amongst its former pupils were Sir Arthur Conan Doyle and Charles Laughton.

As you enter the College grounds from the village there is a very prominent notice informing you that you are entering the Forest of Bowland Area of Outstanding Natural Beauty (AONB) and, somewhat surprisingly perhaps, the grounds which are crossed by several Rights of Way, are open to the general public.

Stonyhurst also houses many treasures including a seventh century copy of St John's Gospel which is said to have belonged to St Cuthbert and a cope of Henry 11 which Henry VIII wore at the famous Field of the Cloth of Gold in northern France where he met the King of France.

There is also an embroidered cap once belonging to St Thomas More, a former Chancellor of England, and a chasuble owned by Queen Catherine of Aragon.

These and other artefacts are on view when the College offers guided tours of the historic rooms and chapels during the month of August (teas and light refreshments are available). For details of opening times, contact the Tourist Information centre, Clitheroe, 01200 25566 or the General Manager, Stonyhurst Development Company, 01254 826345.

The Route

From the road junction in the centre of Hurst Green village take the path immediately to the left of the Shireburn Arms Hotel which is signed, if somewhat obscurely, as a section of the Ribble Way. After a few metres stay to the left of "The Chalet", a small craft shop, to reach a stone step stile which provides an entry to a sloping, uneven field riven by several small streams which act as natural drainage ditches.

Walk to the left of a ditch and a fence as the path loses height rapidly with some fine views of Whalley Nab in the distance ahead. Where the fence terminates continue forward with a stream on your right to reach another Ribble Way sign. By this turn right over a simple footbridge and then make a left turn at once, so continuing down the sloping field along a broad tract of land between a fence on your right and a stream on your left.

A small footbridge with a stile in the middle grants entry into a very sparse woodland. Stay forward over a second footbridge formed by two railway sleepers to a third footbridge accompanied by another Ribble Way sign.

From the far end of this footbridge climb the facing slope while bearing slightly left and passing beneath some overhead wires to reach the end of a row of fence posts which have been relieved of their wires.

Proceed between the posts and a wooded clough on the left. Descend to a wooden stile to enter a small woodland consisting principally of holly and coppiced birch festooned with ivy where the stepped path corkscrews down the steep slope towards a robust wooden footbridge provided by Lancashire County Council.

Beyond this leave the wood and proceed some 7 metres to a stile after which the clear and distinct path clings to the northern bank of the Ribble as it flows through a lush valley with mallard gracing the water.

Within a short distance there is a massive stone aqueduct on the right which carries two enormous pipes across the river and, in the far distance ahead, are the slopes of Pendle Hill. In Spring and early

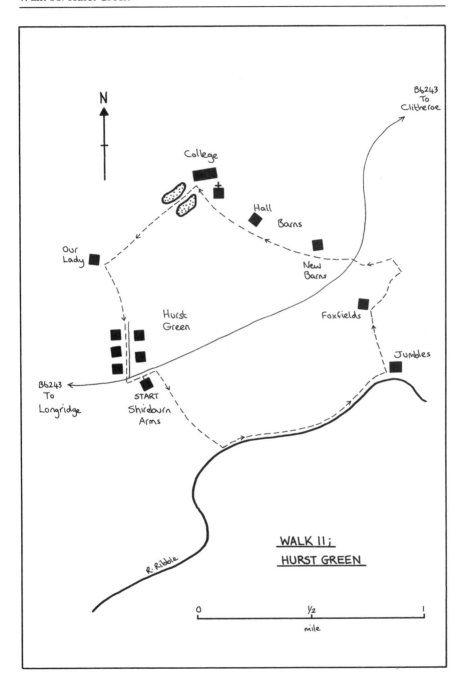

WALK 11;
HURST GREEN

Summer the surrounding pastures provide nesting grounds for curlew and lapwing.

Negotiate the stile at the end of the aqueduct, turn right for 10 metres and then left. still following the riverside path as it skirts the boundary of a cultivated field. After following the boundary of a second arable field the path reaches a stile. Continue along the same line of direction across the following pasture, cross a small footbridge and negotiate another stile to proceed, still along the river bank, until meeting a Ribble Way sign.

This stands where the riverside path forms a junction with a broad track coming from Jumbles Farm which is but a short distance ahead. However, it is not on our route.

Instead, turn left along the track. This soon passes under some overhead wires and crosses a cattle grid before developing into a hedged lane leading to Fox Fields Farm.

Follow the lane as it passes the farmhouse and outbuildings and acquires a metalled surface.

Before an ever-open five-barred gate, once white but now mottled with rust, there is a small overgrown conifer plantation on the right and a stream on the left. Where the lane reaches a small stone cottage carrying the date, 1898, turn left through a metal five-barred gate onto an unsigned and indistinct path which climbs the meadow to the right of a stream and a hedge.

On gaining the field corner, turn left through a five-barred gate and walk alongside the hedge on the right for approximately 60 metres before making a right turn through another gate onto the B6243.

Turn left along the road, walking some 50 metres along the pavement. Turn right and cross the road to a footpath sign accompanied by a stile. Over this follow the broad track which runs close to the hedge on your right before passing, firstly New Barns and, secondly, Loach Field Wood.

Eventually hedgerows appear on both sides of the track as it approaches Hall Barns. By the far end of these negotiate a narrow metal gate to continue along the surfaced lane as it passes rugby pitches and the Observatories before curving right by St Peter's Church.

On reaching the intersection in front of the main entrance to Stony-hurst College turn left to follow the main drive as it passes between the two ornamental lakes and over the parkland to the statue of Our Lady. By this turn left, with the drive, to enter Hurst Green village.

Walk 12: Ribchester

This walk combines field paths with bridleways to provide a delightful excursion from the Roman fort at Ribchester through the rich pastures of the Ribble Valley. It involves only a small amount of gentle climbing but offers rewarding long distance views of Pendle Hill and Longridge Fell.

Route: Ribchester – Parsonage Farm – Ox Hey Farm – Hothersall Hall – Boat House – Lower Barn Farm – Ribchester.

Start: Car park, Ribchester. Map reference 649352.

Distance: 4½ miles (7km)

Map: "Great Harwood and Longridge", number 680 in the O.S. "Pathfinder" series.

Public Transport: Frequent daily buses from Preston, Longridge and Blackburn. Restricted Sunday service. Phone: 01254 681120 or 01772 556818.

By car: Leave the A59, Preston to Skipton road, at Copster Green and follow the road signed to Ribchester. There is a large car park for visitors.

The Tea Shop

The village Tea Shop is centrally situated on Water Street. Opened in 1989 by John and Sandra Jardine, it also combines a craft shop. The intimate atmosphere and warm welcome are both matched by superb home-baking.

The Ribchester Afternoon Tea is of such gigantic proportions that a grease-proof bag is offered in case you wish to take your cake away with you. The choice of cakes is bewildering, everything from melt-in-the-mouth Coffee and Walnut cake to warmed Chocolate Fudge and including Lemon Cake, Deep Egg Custard and Hot Sticky Toffee Pudding. Opt for a simple scone and it will be served with lashings of cream and jam. Another alternative is any one of a wide selection of fruit pies. Toasted teacakes, crumpets oozing butter and even toasted scones are also available.

There are seven different coffees on offer, all differing in strength and served in cafetières. There is an even longer list of speciality teas ranging from English Breakfast to Lapsang Souchong and embracing Earl Grey, Darjeeling and Assam, not to mention the fruit varieties of Peppermint, Wild Strawberry, Lime and Lemon, and Camomile to name but a few.

The village tea shop, Ribchester

For that break in the middle of the day when something rather more substantial is required there are sandwiches, baked potatoes and such dishes as Ribchester Ploughman's and Ribchester Doorstep which consists of a local sausage on a toasted tea cake served with mustard or Cranberry Sauce.

Opening Times: Summer: Wednesday, Thursday and Friday, 11.am to 5.pm. Saturday and Sunday, 10.30am to 5.30pm. Winter: Open Fridays, Saturdays and Sundays only. Hours as above. **Phone:** 01254 878297.

The Village

Ribchester, one of the most interesting villages in the Ribble Valley, has had a long and chequered history. People have occupied the site since the Bronze Age as was revealed by the discovery of Bronze Age burial urns in 1977 when the car park was under construction.

In turn it became a Roman Fort but then descended into obscurity during the Dark Ages. However, there is a suspicion that a church was built at some time before the Norman Conquest although no mention is made of one in the Domesday Book of 1086.

In 1322 Ribchester was attacked and pillaged by Robert the Bruce leading a party of Scottish raiders and more than 100 inhabitants fell victim to the Black Death in the fourteenth century. After that little of note happened in Ribchester until the Civil War when the Earl of Derby passed through with a party of looting Cavaliers and, later, several locals supported the Jacobites in their Rebellion of 1715.

Ribchester developed economically during the eighteenth century when handloom weaving became the staple industry. Many of the attractive stone houses standing along the main street and Water Lane were built as weavers' cottages. During the same period several mills were built for the turning of bobbins, then in great demand for the cotton industry.

The advent of the Industrial Revolution brought this economic boom to an end but the late twentieth century has witnessed a revival sparked-off by the rapid growth in tourism. People are attracted by the Roman remains, the church of St Wilfrid and the general atmosphere of the village itself. It tends to become crowded at week-ends and on Bank Holidays.

The Roman Museum

Ribchester is the only village to stand on the banks of the Ribble, a river notorious for changing its course. Over the centuries this has led to the loss of a large area of the Roman Fort which was constructed in AD 79 to protect the roads from Manchester to Carlisle and from York to another Roman base on the coast near Fleetwood.

It covered approximately six acres and provided accommodation for 500 cavalry and their horses. The original contingent came from northern Spain but these were later replaced by troops from Rumania.

Several important excavations of the site have been made and many of the artefacts unearthed are to be found in the small museum, opened in 1914, which stands in the very centre of the fort area. Collections of coins, pottery, especially Samian ware, brooches, leatherwork and other relics are imaginatively displayed alongside models of the fort and the civilian houses which occupied the area immediately outside.

Opening Times: All year: Monday to Friday, 9am to 5pm. Saturday and Sunday: 12am to 5pm.

The Route

Begin by walking away from the village along the surfaced road which runs between the car park on your right and the playing fields on your left. By the end of the car park a notice announces that this is a private road but a bridleway sign also confirms that it is open for walkers. The square-towered parish church is a short distance away to your left beyond the playing fields.

Approximately 50 metres beyond the end of the car park the road bends left through ninety degrees but, almost at once, swings right, soon crossing a cattle grid situated between two short low stretches of drystone walling.

Where the road bends to the right ignore an obvious stile on your left, staying forward through a white metal five-barred gate. By a green caravan follow the bridleway to the left and climb a short, steep hill before reaching a house.

By the far corner of this turn left for 10 metres but, before reaching Parsonage Farm, and directed by a black and white footpath sign, turn right to negotiate a wooden five-barred gate. Within a few yards turn right through a second gate and then turn left immediately.

Climbing almost imperceptibly, stay to the right of a hedge along the field boundary to a wooden stile. With Longridge Fell clearly visible on your right, go forward while aiming for a small wooden gate, alongside one of the five-barred variety in the facing hedge.

Through this veer leftwards across the ensuing large field, aiming for the corner and a waymarked five-barred gate. Advance between a hedge on your left and a wire fence on your right for approximately 100 metres to a rusty gate where there is a pond on your left.

Continue straight ahead over the next very large field with Eatough's Wood, which is partly coniferous, some distance away to your right. The path is somewhat indistinct in places so aim for a small copse of trees surrounding another pond.

This is a surprisingly idyllic spot where, in winter, redwings and fieldfares abound. It also makes an ideal point for a short coffee break.

Stay to the left of the pond before veering slightly left towards a small metal gate which, initially, is not visible because it lies in a depression in the ground. Through this gate climb slightly to a more distinct path with a stream on your right. Once the path fades on the ground head for a gateway with a partially white stile adjacent.

Beyond this maintain direction towards the right-hand corner of a stone house in the distance, the stream moving further away to the right. The path passes through a gateway, recognised by some silver plastic sheeting alongside. Beyond, the path widens as it stays close to a fence on your left to reach a metal five-barred gate by Ox Hey Farm. This gate provides access onto a bridleway.

Turn left, shortly passing through a very tall wire gate and beneath some overhead power lines. Beyond the next bend the lane acquires a

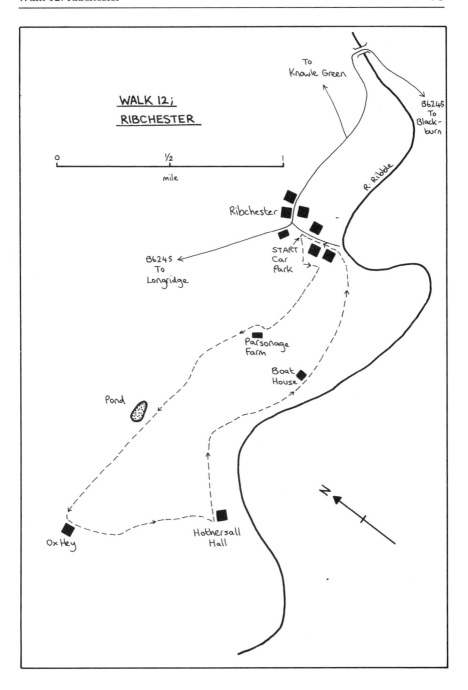

grass surface until reaching another wire gate. Through this the path again becomes somewhat indistinct so maintain direction towards a fence corner.

Pass through a gateway with a splendid view of the Ribble down below. From the next fence corner cross the centre of the field to another gate beyond which the bridleway becomes a concrete track as it loses height towards Hothersall Hall.

Through the next gate, which is waymarked, turn left along a broad track which leads directly to the imposing stone house which is Hothersall Hall. Built in 1695, this was the home of Sir John Hothersall who was outlawed for his part in the 1715 Jacobite Rebellion. Today it is the property of the Robinson family who farm the surrounding land.

Follow the waymarks which lead you round to the left of the house to enter a fenced lane which is a part of the Ribble Way. 250 metres beyond Hothersall Hall, where the lane bends sharply to the left, turn right over a ladder stile recognisable by the Ribble Way sign, and climb the steep path to the top of Red Bank. This affords a fine view of the Ribble as it meanders through the pastoral landscape.

At the top of Red Bank swing right, so keeping to the edge of the escarpment and a little to the left of the trees, guided by the occasional waymark. Eventually a track, its course delineated by large, square stones is reached.

Do not use it. Instead, swing round further to the right, staying close to the trees for the descent of the steep hillside to reach a wooden kissing gate at river level.

Continue forward to the left of a fence and over a stile which is followed, in due course, by a gateway. After that the route develops into a wide track passing between hedgerows with the Ribble but a short distance to the right.

Pass the Boat House, a white building on your left that served as the home of the man who operated the ferry at this point until about 50 years ago.

A short distance beyond comes Lower Barn Farm, a sturdy stone house which has recently been restored. Remain along this hedged lane until it passes through the yard of Lower Alston Farm. From the farm gate it acquires a metalled surface as it continues by the Roman Museum and the Church of St Wilfrid, both on the left.

From the Museum follow the road into the village for approximately 100 metres before turning left into the car park.

Walk 13: Waddington

A short, gentle route mainly along field paths with some fine views of the Bowland Fells.

Route: Waddington – King Henry's Grove – Hollins Clough – Gannies Farm – Lower New House – Pinder Hill – Waddington.

Start: Waddington village. Map reference 729438.

Distance: 3 miles (4.8km)

Map: "Forest of Bowland and Ribblesdale", number 41 in the O.S. "Outdoor Leisure" series.

Public Transport: There are several buses daily from Clitheroe, Settle and Slaidburn. On Summer Sundays and Bank Holidays there are Leisure Link services from Nelson, Clitheroe, Morecambe, Lancaster, Chorley, Preston and Burnley.

By car: Waddington village is on the B6478 two miles north of Clitheroe. There is no car park but several spots for off-road parking.

The Tea Shop

The ever popular Country Kitchen Tea Shop in Waddington has all the hallmarks of a former village shop with its large windows. A touch of luxury is provided by the glass-topped tables with their pink and white lace tablecloths.

Owner Tim Slater insists that the food he provides is made on the premises, so guaranteeing its quality. His scones, with preserves and cream, or even just with butter, melt in the mouth invariably creating a desire for a second.

Not that scones are the only temptation. Apple Sultana Cake or Sticky Toffee Pudding, served hot with cream, tempt many walkers at the end of their day. So, too, do the Carrot Cake, Chocolate Fudge Cake and Fruit and Bran Loaf.

The Country Kitchen also serves a wide range of light lunches and snacks including Steak and Kidney Pie, Cheese and Onion Pie along with sandwiches and jacket potatoes. There is also a choice of speciality teas and coffees.

Opening Times: Tuesday to Sunday (all year) 10am to 4.30pm. Closed Mondays except Bank Holidays. **Phone:** 01200 429364.

Country Kitchen tea rooms, Waddington

Waddington

Waddington's principal attraction is to be found in the gardens which line Waddington Brook as it flows through the village street. It takes its name from its traditional founder, Wadda, an Anglo-Saxon chieftain. The church, dedicated to St Helen, the mother of the Roman Emperor Augustus and the discoverer of the True Cross, still retains its sixteenth century tower although the remainder of the building dates from 1901. Outside the church are the stocks. Also of note is Waddington Hall which stands almost next to the Country Kitchen. Over the gateway are carved the words, "I will raise up his ruins and I will build as in the days of old."

In 1900 John Waddington restored the Hall to its former glory when it had served as the manor house of the Tempest family. During the Wars of the Roses King Henry VI sheltered there but his enemies discovered his whereabouts and, as they approached, he escaped through the dining room window.

The Route

From the centre of Waddington take the road which passes the church and is signed to Mitton and Bashall Eaves. By the Buck Inn, located on a sharp left-hand bend, stay forward along a narrow surfaced road signed as a public footpath to Bashall Eaves.

After a few metres, and by the entrance to a house bearing the unusual

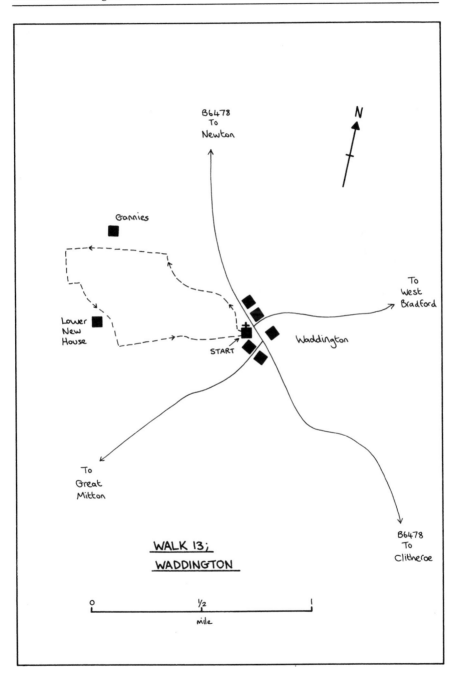

B6478
To
Newton

N

Gannies

To
West
Bradford

Lower
New
House

START

Waddington

To
Great
Mitton

B6478
To
Clitheroe

WALK 13;
WADDINGTON

0 ½ 1
mile

name of "The Roost", turn right, as directed by another sign. "Beech-thorpe Barn", converted into a house, is on your right. After 100 metres pass through a small white gate and, ten metres further, turn left over a well-worn stone footbridge. Immediately make a right turn to a stone step stile and follow the distinct path as it makes its way through some trees. Eventually another stone step stile is negotiated alongside a length of stone wall.

By an old corrugated-iron shed the path swings towards the left as it traverses a very large field towards the corner of a fence. Stay to the right of the fence to a stile set deeply into the facing hedgerow.

Maintain your direction to the left of a hedge to a metal five-barred gate which is almost in the field corner. Cross the subsequent field by veering leftwards to reach a stile set amongst some tall deciduous trees. Hollin's Farm is but a short distance to your right. This area is shown on the map as "King Henry's Grove", an obvious reference to the monarch's stay at Waddington Hall.

Over this stile turn right to follow the path into Hollin's Clough. This is well wooded and also boasts several very large patches of nettles. Where the path meets a wide track turn left to pass an overhead pipe on your right. Simultaneously the track swings left to cross a stone bridge. From the bridge advance to a metal five-barred gate.

Through this the track narrows to a path which passes beneath some overhead wires and keeps just to the left of a wire fence before reaching a wooden stile in the field corner. It then proceeds immediately to the left of a well-trimmed hawthorn hedge. Where this veers ever so slightly to the right, stay forward to a solitary wooden gate post and another fence corner. By this corner, turn left to reach a wooden footbridge. At the far end, with Gannies Farm away to your right, stay forward across the field to another wooden stile. This provides access to a chatter track that is not shown on the Ordnance Survey map because it has only recently been constructed.

Turn left along this and gradually lose height to a T-junction. Lower New House Farm is a short distance to your right. Make another left turn, cross another stone bridge and go through a metal five-barred gate. Beyond this the path stays to the left of a hedge as it passes through another gate. Waddington church tower comes into view ahead.

Stay to the left of a barn, reminiscent of so many in the Yorkshire Dales, while negotiating a five-barred gate alongside. The path, now a delightful grassy track, passes between two gaunt dead trees while staying to the left of a wall beyond which is Pinder Hill.

Another gate is followed by a blocked cattle grid and, some 200 metres beyond, the route enters Waddington village, passing to the left of the parish church as it returns to the Country Kitchen.

Walk 14: Mill Lane

Using a mixture of field paths and lanes, this route climbs onto the slopes of Waddington Fell before returning to the centre of the village.

Route: Waddington – Eaves House – Old Town Head – Eaves Hall – Seedalls – Mill Lane – Dovecote – Feazer Wood – Waddington.

Start: Waddington village. Map reference 729438.

Distance: 4½ miles (7km).

Map: "Forest of Bowland and Ribblesdale", number 41 in the O.S. "Outdoor Leisure" series.

Public Transport: Waddington has several buses daily from Clitheroe, Settle and Slaidburn. On Summer Sundays and Bank Holidays it is served by the Leisure Link buses from Clitheroe, Morecambe, Lancaster, Chorley, Darwen, Preston, Ormskirk, Blackpool, Nelson, and Burnley.

By car: Waddington is two miles north of Clitheroe on the B6478. There is no car park in the village but several places for off-road parking.

The Tea Shop

Situated on Mill Lane, about one mile north of Waddington village, the Dovecote Tea Rooms command a fine view out over the Ribble Valley. They are housed in a modern bungalow with a large sliding window leading out onto the patio and into the garden where several extra tables are available when the weather is suitable. Inside, the white walls are decorated with water colours and the sideboard boasts a fine collection of foreign currency notes, ornamental tea pots and royal souvenir plates.

All the mouth-watering cakes are home made on the premises and so, too, are the Apple Pie, Custard Tart, Rhubarb Crumble and Gooseberry Crumble. They are served with generous portions of cream or ice-cream according to taste. For something even a little richer there is Banana Split, Toffee Cream Meringue or Danish Apple Desert. As an alternative there is Afternoon Tea.

For anyone anxious to avoid such temptations the Dovecote also offers a variety of sandwiches, both ordinary or toasted, salads and jacket potatoes. Hot dishes include Cheese and Onion Pie, Hot Pot with Red Cabbage or Chicken, Ham and Mushroom Pie accompanied by Mushy Peas.

The Dovecote

Speciality teas include Assam, Ceylon, Earl Grey and Fruit. For those with a different taste there is freshly ground Colombian coffee, hot chocolate, fresh milk or soft drinks.

Opening Times: Daily all year, 10am to 6pm. Closed Mondays except Bank Holidays. **Phone:** 01200 23033.

The Route

From the village centre take the road signed to West Bradford, passing Waddington Hospital on your left. This institution was endowed in 1709 by Robert Parker of Morley Hall in Yorkshire for "the reception of poor widows" and is still in use today.

By a footpath sign at the far corner of the hospital turn left and then immediately right through a five-barred gate to enter a farmyard. After about ten metres turn left by the first barn to negotiate a second five-barred gate into a field.

Cross on the clear track to the diagonally opposite corner and pass through another wooden five-barred gate. Continue just to the left of a fence.

Where this corners, veer slightly to the left with the vague path as it climbs the open field to reach a wooden footbridge spanning a stream in a shallow clough. At the far end of this footbridge maintain a leftwards direction as you continue climbing gently towards Eaves House which is now clearly visible.

Over the stile in the corner of the field just in front of the house, turn left along the driveway. Advance for a few metres. Immediately in front of Eaves House stay along the metalled track as it bends to the right and crosses two cattle grids before eventually reaching a double five-barred gate with a stone house just beyond.

Do not go through the gates because there is no right of way. Instead, turn right by a derelict stile and stay close to the house boundary fence which is on the left. Stay alongside it until the corner of the field is reached after a few metres.

In the corner turn right and with a fence on your immediate left, descend the field to the bottom corner.

There, turn left over a stile and walk to the left of another fence. After 100 metres turn right through an old wooden kissing gate set into the fence, negotiate the facing stile and turn left thereby maintaining the same direction but now to the right of a fence.

In the next field corner descend a shallow bank to cross a stream, turn right and keep a fence on your left for ten metres before turning left over a wooden footbridge.

From this cross the centre of the next field to a fence corner before maintaining the same bearing for 70 metres to the right of the fence to reach an ancient metal kissing gate.

Through this advance to the right of a line of trees for a further 80 metres before descending a flight of ten steps to a footpath sign and Eaves Lane.

Turn left to embark on a long, steep climb for about one mile (1.6km) which will carry you past Eaves Hall, now a country club, Three Rivers Park, Drake House Stables and Hancock's Farm.

Gradually the higher slopes of Waddington Fell come into view a short distance in front and the lane verges are lined with red campion, nettles, brambles, hogweed, ragged robin and birdsfoot trefoil.

Continue climbing until the lane swings through ninety degrees to the left and develops into a bridleway signed to Seedall's Farm.

With this change of direction there is a panoramic view to the left embracing a vast expanse of the Ribble Valley with Pendle Hill beyond.

Pass the white-coloured Seedall's Farmhouse on your right and, by the far end, negotiate a wooden five-barred gate with a footpath sign. The track, now level and grassy, provides excellent walking conditions until it reaches a metal five-barred gate with Cluttock Clough Farm just beyond.

Continue forward along the lane to pass Waddington Old Mill, now a private residence, until reaching the Dovecote Tea Rooms after a further few metres.

Suitably refreshed, retrace your steps to the far corner of Waddington Old Mill. There turn right along another lane which passes between two new stone houses. By a facing five-barred gate just beyond, make a left turn over a stile before turning sharply to the right and walking to the left of a wooden fence.

Descend a short distance, cross a wooden footbridge and then turn immediately to the left for the short climb up the slope. At the top of the rise turn sharply to the right to stay with the right-hand boundary of the field and to the left of Feazer Wood. There is a stream flowing down through the wooded clough on your right.

At this stage the path is very distinct and easy to navigate. Beyond the first stile maintain the same line of direction along the field boundary while losing height to pass to the right of a covered reservoir. A somewhat flimsy stile in the fence in the far right-hand corner of the field allows access onto a rough lane.

Turn left along this. Feazer Farm is a few metres to your left. After ten metres along the lane turn right, as though to enter the woods.

However, after a further ten metres, make a left turn over a stone step stile which is about five metres to the right of a small, low public utility marker bearing the letters,

FWB
MAIN.

On the far side of the stile proceed in the same general direction, still to the left of a fence and of Feazer Woods while losing altitude down a long, narrow field. As the field narrows even further the path becomes more distinct and the clough on the right deepens.

Pass through a metal five-barred metal gate with a stile alongside and then aim for the tower of Waddington church which is now visible ahead. As the path loses even more height in the subsequent field, it leads to a stile in the field corner some four metres to the right of a facing metal five-barred gate.

On the far side initially continue along the track which has developed but, where this moves rightwards towards a solitary caravan, maintain your general direction along a path which passes between a wall on the right and a vastly overgrown hedge on the left.

A stone step stile with a footpath sign alongside is soon reached. Over this, turn right along the road for the final few yards back into the centre of Waddington village.

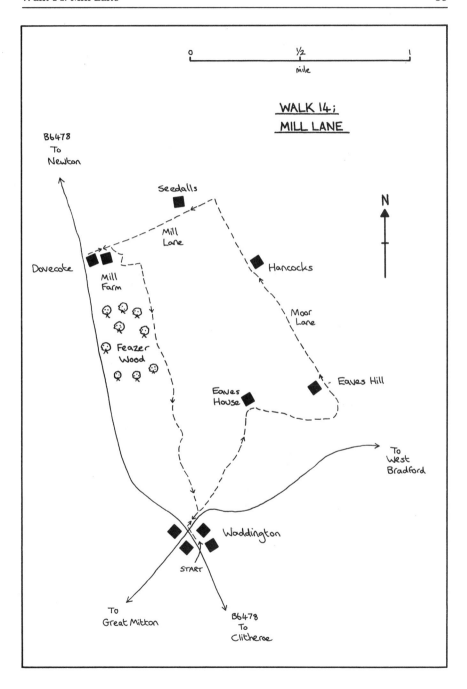

Walk 15: Slaidburn

A route through the heart of Bowland revealing the rich tapestry of its landscape: the lush river valleys, the high fells and attractive stone villages.

Route: Slaidburn – New Laithes – Pain Hill – Crawshaw – Newton –
                     River Hodder – Dunnow Hall – Slaidburn.

Start: The riverside car park, Slaidburn. Map reference 714524.

Distance: 5½ miles (9km).

Map: "Forest of Bowland and Ribblesdale", number 41 in the O.S. "Outdoor
                     Leisure" series.

Public Transport: Slaidburn has daily (except Sundays) buses from Clitheroe. Buses from
                     Settle on Tuesdays. On Summer Sundays and Bank Holidays
                     Slaidburn is served by the Hodder valley Rambler from Blackpool and
                     Preston. Phone 01200 442226 for leaflet and details.

By car: Slaidburn is reached by the B6478 from either Clitheroe on the A59 or
                     Long Preston on the A65. From Lancaster and the north it may be
                     reached by taking the A683 towards Kirkby Lonsdale and turning right
                     onto the signed but unclassified road at Caton and following it through
                     the Trough of Bowland, Dunsop Bridge and Newton.

The Tea Shop

As it name suggests, the Riverbank Tea Rooms in Slaidburn overlooks the sparkling waters of the River Hodder. It also has the great benefit of standing adjacent to the car park so it is the ideal venue at the end of the day.

The café itself is upstairs. The upper half of the walls is cream, matched by a floral pattern on the lower half. It is small with a cosy, intimate atmosphere. Downstairs is an equally small snack bar and, for those warm, balmy days of high summer, there are tables outside facing the village green.

The menu poses problems requiring difficult choices. There are Cream Teas and Afternoon Teas along with such delicious temptations as Brandied Black Cherry Meringue, Banana Toffee Pie, Strawberry Meringue and an amazing display of home-made fruit pies.

Anyone with a larger appetite can try the Cheese and Onion Pie,

Mixed Grill, Minced Beef and Vegetable Pie, home-made Lasagne or the various specials that are there to tempt your taste buds. There is the usual selection of beverages. Suffice it to say that the Riverbank caters for all sizes of appetite and the emphasis is on quality.

Opening Times: Daily (except Christmas Day) 10.30am to 5pm. **Phone:** 01200 446398.

Slaidburn

Slaidburn, the principal village of the Hodder Valley, lies in the very heart of Bowland and, until the 1974 boundary changes, belonged to Yorkshire. Its transfer to Lancashire in that year almost caused civil war and was deeply resented by many of the local inhabitants.

The village is a most attractive collection of stone houses and cottages with old-fashioned pebbled pavements which has managed to avoid the excesses of modernisation. The Green, always popular with visitors, lies at the eastern end of the village by the elegant stone bridge spanning the River Hodder, surely the most delightful of all Lancashire's waterways. The church stands alongside the road to Newton adjacent to an early seventeenth century Grammar School which still serves as the Slaidburn Primary.

The 'Hark to Bounty'

The heart of the village, where three roads meet, is dominated by a cluster of buildings – the Post Office and general store, the Youth Hostel and the "Hark to Bounty" Inn. Originally the pub was the location for the court which exercised jurisdiction over the entire Forest of Bowland which enjoyed its own strict code of laws governing hunting, poaching and land rights.

The unusual name of the pub is alleged by local tradition to be derived from an incident in the nineteenth century when a visiting huntsman heard the cry of a celebrated hound and yelled, "Hark to Bounty".

It is a reminder to the summer visitor that Bowland comes alive during the autumn and winter with the sound of the huntsman's horn. This traditional country sport is followed enthusiastically by the Pendle Forest and Craven Hunt. Otter hunts were once a prominent feature of local life but in recent years these delightful creatures have been placed on the endangered list. Consequently the otter hunts now focus their attention on the evasive mink, an alien species which, having escaped from their farms, prey on our declining riparian wildlife.

The Church of St Andrew is perched on raised ground as you enter the village from Newton. It is low and squat, with a square tower. Built in the fifteenth century, it remains almost unaltered. The highlight is the Jacobean rood screen installed during the reign of Charles I when it was official government policy for services to revert to the pre-Reformation style. It is unique in Lancashire. Another unusual feature is the three-decker pulpit while the nave is filled with seventeenth century and Georgian box-pews, all of which escaped the "improvements" of the Victorians.

The Route

Leaving the riverside car park, turn right along the road to pass the Riverbank Tea Rooms followed by several stone cottages before climbing by the dignified War Memorial. On reaching the T-junction by the "Hark to Bounty", continue forwards along the minor road which passes more cottages before embarking on a steep climb of one-in-eight.

Where the gradient levels New Laithes is reached on the left. Surprisingly there is no footpath sign at this point but, by the far end of the buildings, make a left turn through a five-barred gate onto a track.

Initially this clings close to the wall on your left but, beyond a cattle grid, the wall terminates while the track continues. It gradually climbs across open pastures filled with the sounds of bleating sheep and in Spring and early Summer curlews and lapwing add their voices to this natural chorus.

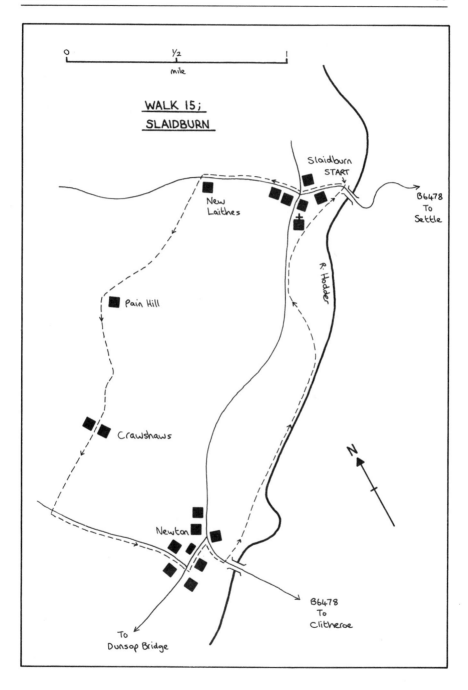

The extensive view opens up to reveal the higher moorlands of Bowland to your right including Low Fell, Burn Fell and Dunsop Fell with Croasdale in the further distance. On the left there are glimpses of Great Dunnow Hill which is much closer to hand.

Cross a second cattle grid and, some distance beyond, negotiate a wooden five-barred gate to follow the track between the buildings of Pain Hill Farm. In the middle of these, as instructed by a painted notice, turn right to another gate.

Immediately through this turn sharply to the left, following the clear path a little to the right of another wall until reaching a stone step stile adjacent to a five-barred gate in the corner of the field.

Continue forwards along a curving green swathe which runs to the left of a small clump of trees until meeting a wall. Turn right and, keeping the wall on your left, maintain the gradual climb until arriving at a stone step stile by another five-barred gate.

Stay forward, passing to the right of the house at Crawshaw Farm and then following the track for several hundred metres until it forms a junction with Back Lane, a surfaced minor lane leading to Higher Wood House.

Turn left along this for the steep descent into the village of Newton. The former Friends Meeting House stands on your left by the entrance to the village. This was in continuous use as a place of worship from 1776 until 1988.

At the T-junction a few metres beyond make a left turn. Within a few metres there is a second junction. Turn right for the descent of the short hill by the Parkers Arms and, continuing along the road towards Clitheroe for one hundred metres, reach the stone bridge spanning the River Hodder.

By the near-end of this and by the traffic de-restriction signs, turn left through a small wooden gate to cross the tiny meadow on a distinct path with the crystal clear waters of the Hodder on your right.

Negotiate a second wooden gate, descend a small flight of steps and proceed along the delightful riverside path through a small wood to a third wicket gate distinguished by a waymarker sign.

Still maintaining the same direction, remain to the left of a wall before swinging right over a stone slab footbridge to yet another small wooden gate. Through this turn left and, with another wall on your left initially, followed by a fence and stream, proceed along the field boundary until coming to a stile a your left.

Negotiate this and turn immediately to the right to continue in the same direction along a grass belvedere just inside the perimeter of a wood and a few feet above the Hodder. Leave the wood by a metal kissing gate to cross the largest of the riverside meadows, staying close to the base of the steep and well-wooded slope of Great Dunnow Hill.

Path and river soon diverge but, by the gaunt Great Dunnow Hall, the path forms an inverted Y-junction with another track coming from a footbridge over the river to your right. Ignore this and stay forward along the wide track, soon passing an electricity sub-station by a 3-fingered footpath post.

Continue forward through a five-barred gate and follow the track until a small metal gate affords access onto the Slaidburn to Newton road by "The Lodge".

Turn right along the road, very quickly meeting the first houses on the outskirts of Slaidburn. By the village sign turn right up a small flight of stone steps and then left through a metal kissing gate to enter the churchyard.

Advance to the left of a sundial and, a few metres beyond, of a small area enclosed by iron railings. Pass the East end of the church and then stay to the right of the village school before going through a small wooden gate. Continue for a few metres to a metal kissing gate and then maintain the same bearing over the ensuing field whilst staying to the right of the hedge which surrounds the school playground.

Where the hedge corners to the left, bear left with the distinct path to pass a square stone structure on your right. This is shown on the map as a well. A few metres beyond is a waymarker post. Follow the direction of the arrow to negotiate another small wicket gate before turning left so that the Hodder is once again on your right. Cross the village green to the café and car park.

Walk 16: Chipping

A route along field paths and green lanes, which leads into the heart of the Bowland Fells where silence and solitude reign.

Route: Chipping – Birchen Lee – Windy Hill Farm – High Barns – Burnslack –
                   Ward's End – Saddle End – Bradley – Nan King's Farm – Chipping.

Start: Car park, Chipping. Map reference 622433.

Distance: 6 miles (9.5km).

Map: "The Forest of Bowland and Ribblesdale", number 41 in the O.S.
                   "Outdoor Leisure" series.

Public Transport: Chipping is served by frequent daily (except Sundays) buses from
                   Clitheroe and Longridge. On Summer Sundays and Bank Holidays
                   there are leisure link buses from Chorley, Leyland, Preston, Blackpool
                   and Ormskirk.

By car: Chipping is located at the centre of a web of unclassified roads. It is best
                   approached from the A6 at Broughton by way of Longridge (signed) or
                   from Clitheroe (signed). There is a car park close to the church.

The Tea Shop

The Cobbled Corner Cafe, standing near the church in Chipping, provides a warm welcome and a cosy atmosphere for anyone who has spent a day walking the surrounding fells. The centre of the room is dominated by an isolated chimney breast complete with an old-fashioned iron stove set into its fireplace.

The decor is mixed, the walls housing displays of pictures which are for sale and dried flower arrangements. One area of the floor is quarry tiled. The tables, with their lace cloths, are surrounded by fine examples of Berry's chairs.

The speciality of the house is "Bungo Soup", so-called "because everything is bunged in". The "Bikers' Favourite" consists of beans on toast, egg on toast or sausage roll. There is an extensive offering of sandwiches, toasties, omelets and jacket potatoes. For those who are ravenously famished there is one real Lancashire speciality – corned beef hotpot with red cabbage.

The cakes are "for those with no will power". They are offered a choice, amongst many others, of the Cobbled Corner's "famous carrot

The Cobbled Corner Cafe

cake which is known for miles around", Egg Custard, fruit pies, currant slices, scones or Coffee Cake. All are baked on the premises.

Opening Times: Daily all year, 10am to 5pm (closed Christmas Day). **Phone:** 01995 61551.

Chipping

The name "Chipping" is said to be derived from the early English "Cepping", meaning "Market Place". There is no market in Chipping today but from the earliest recorded times Chipping has served the needs and requirements of those families who have carved their farms and a precarious livelihood out of the lower slopes of the Bowland Fells.

Until the middle of the nineteenth century the village boasted two very important fairs each year where cattle and other goods were bought and sold. As early as the middle of the fourteenth century the Abbot of Whalley wrote that Chipping was "in a manner inaccessible to man". While this no longer holds true, the village is not easy to reach.

Until the seventeenth century Chipping was the focus of an agrarian community but at about that date the textile industry started to develop, resulting in the foundation of several mills operating along Chipping Brook. These vanished long ago, the main industry now being the production of wooden chairs by Berry's.

Several of the cottages and houses lining the streets date from the seventeenth and eighteenth centuries, many still carrying the dates of their construction. Notable buildings include St Mary's Catholic Church and the almshouses and school endowed by John Brabin whose former home now serves as the Post Office.

The "Sun Inn" is reputedly haunted by the ghost of Lizzie Dean who, on being jilted, took her own life. The parish church of St Bartholomew is believed to have been founded shortly prior to the Norman Conquest although the oldest surviving parts only date from the fourteenth and fifteenth centuries.

The Route

Exit the car park by the entrance facing St Bartholomew's Church and turn left along Church Rake. After some 200 metres, and by a set of white iron railings, fork right down a minor road to pass Berry's chair-making factory on your right and the former workhouse on your left. Beyond Grove Square, recognised by the piles of timber, swing right over a stone bridge before climbing slightly to Mill Pond. Now a small haven for wildlife, this formerly supplied the factory with its motive power. Opposite this, and by a footpath sign, turn right into the driveway to Austin House, once owned by the Leagram Estate but now belonging to Berry's.

After ten metres, and before a facing wooden gate, make a right turn over a waymarked stile. Heading some 45 degrees to the left, climb the grassy slope on the clear path to pass beneath two sets of overhead wires. Eventually the path meets a fence and turns left. As the going eases, pass through a row of windswept hawthorns with views of Parlick and other fells away to your left.

Negotiate a stile to enter an extremely large field which appears devoid of landmarks and where the path becomes somewhat indistinct. Go under more overhead wires and veer leftwards, away from the long row of pylons which stretches ahead and gradually draw closer to a clough on your left.

Eventually a waymarker offers a choice of two routes. Select the path which moves away to the left while staying to the right of a small abandoned quarry before reaching a wooden stile located between the end of a fence on the left and a stone wall on the right. Leagram Hall, where Catholics once gathered to hear Mass in secret, is hidden by the trees to your right.

On the far side of this stile maintain direction towards a fence corner, first crossing a stream and then continuing alongside the fence as the path becomes more obvious while heading towards a stile located in the field corner.

This stile provides access onto a concrete track. Turn left, pass Birchen Lee Farm while staying to the right of the outbuildings. Where the concrete terminates, continue forward along the rough track, passing first through a wooden five-barred gate and, after a further 250 metres, one of the metal variety.

This leads into the yard of Windy Hill Farm. However, *do not* proceed as far as the house. Instead, once through the gate, turn sharply right as suggested by a waymark which also indicates a path to Burnslack. Keeping a stone barn on your left, advance a few metres to a five-barred gate and then continue climbing along a partially sunken green lane.

After a short distance the gradient eases and the lane narrows into a path running to the left of a fence towards a stile in the right-hand corner of the field. Continue along the same bearing to reach another way-marked stile. In the following field, walk only as far as the end of the first corner of the wall. There, bear left while contouring around the base of the small hillock on your right to reach a stile in the facing fence. Over that maintain direction over the next field to a stile by a wooden footpath finger post at Barn End. This stile allows access to a wide track.

Turn right along this track as it penetrates deeper and deeper into the heart of the fells with Burnslack Fell directly ahead and Saddle Fell gradually coming into the picture when you reach a height of 256 metres or 800 feet.

After the first cattle grid the going levels. The track crosses a second grid before reaching a gate bearing a sign, "Footpath Only", in front of Burnslack House. This is a substantial stone affair surrounded by a shelter-belt of wind-blown trees. Pass through this gate and stay to the left of the house, cornering it round to the right as directed by a large, red-lettered footpath sign to reach a wooden five-barred gate. Through this, and by an Open Access Area sign, turn sharply to the left and, staying just to the right of a stone wall, proceed to the very base of Saddle Fell and another Open Access Area sign.

The atmosphere in this quiet, remote area of the Bowland Fells is somewhat reminiscent of that to be found in such Scottish valleys as Glen Roy. It is certainly a spot in which to pause, to sit, to admire and to contemplate about the beauty of nature and the meaning of life. It is a place for spiritual re-fuelling.

By the second Open Access Area sign turn sharply to the left, cross a planked wooden footbridge to a stile and then advance to the immediate left of a wall as the path stays along the contours of the flanks of Saddle Fell.

Soon the delightful grassy track climbs to pass firstly the ruins of a farm and, subsequently, to reach a barn. Pass to the right of this and the ensuing wall for a further climb with a panoramic vista out over the Ribble Valley gradually opening-up away to your left. To the right are the gorse-covered slopes of Saddle Fell.

Where the accompanying wall on your left terminates, keep forward on a slightly wider track which soon loses height to reach a stile and, a few metres beyond, a 3-fingered footpath post by Saddle End Farm. Turn left along the concreted track signed to Chipping, pass through a metal five-barred gate and stay to the left of the house.

By the end of the wall on the right and a pylon, make a right turn over a waymarked stile, advancing some twelve metres to a waymarked post. Turn left there through a young plantation and continue to the left of a fence along a distinct path until reaching another waymarked stile.

Over that veer left over a footbridge composed of two railway sleepers to reach another stile after 50 metres. Cross the subsequent large field by staying initially to the right of a fence whilst aiming a shade to the left of Bradley Barn which is clearly visible. The Christmas Pudding shape of Parlick is now close-by on your right.

Where the fence corners away, continue directly ahead to a stile by a footpath post at the corner of Bradley Barn. This allows access to a minor road.

Turn right but, after 150 metres and part of the way down a small hill, turn left into the mouth of the driveway to Peacock Hey Farm. Do not use the drive. Instead make a right turn over a stile and take your direction from the arm of the footpath post, aiming for the end of a patch of overgrown scrubland on the left.

By this corner, and following the distinct path, swing left and pass beneath overhead wires towards the visible roof of Nan King's Farm. By the farm buildings turn left, as shown by a waymark, and work your way round the building to spot a yellow waymark on the trunk of a tree.

Guided by this, traverse the first field to a stile in a facing wire fence. Again turn right, as indicated by a home-made footpath sign, and pass through some trees with a fence on the right until reaching yet another stile. Over this turn left and cross a narrow field to an obvious stile by a wooden five-barred gate.

Turn left to walk between two wire fences for a distance of 20 metres to yet another stile and then stay forward along the field boundary to another home-made footpath sign. Here, turn right over an old ladder stile before veering to the left and aiming for a stile bearing a crudely painted yellow arrow. Stay to the left of a fence while losing altitude until reaching a footpath sign by a road. Turn left along this to pass, after some 30 metres, the Mill Pond before completing your walk into the centre of Chipping.

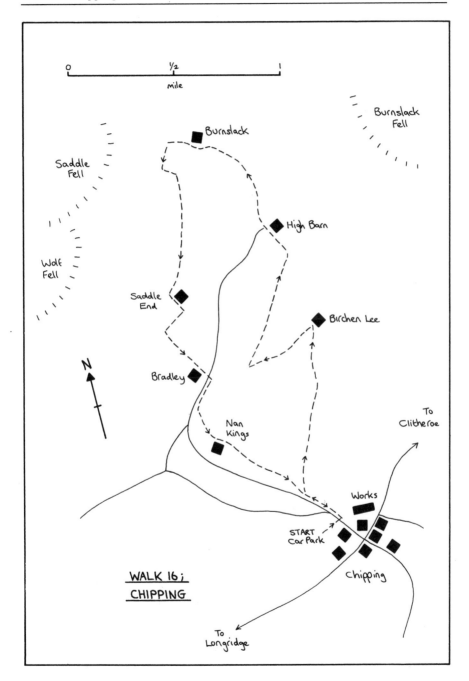

WALK 16;
CHIPPING

Walk 17: Bleasdale

Starting high on Beacon Fell at 266 metres (700 feet), this route descends into the plain around Bleasdale before visiting the church of Saint Eadmer and swinging west to follow the course of the River Brock. It uses mainly field paths and lanes.

Route: Beacon Fell Country Park – Dog and Partridge – Bailey Hey –
                        Bleasdale Post Office – Bleasdale School – St Eadmer's Church –
                        New Bridge Wood – Gill Barn Wood – Heatherway Farm – Broadhead
                        Farm – Beacon Fell Country Park.

Start: The Quarry Car Park, Beacon Fell Country Park. Map reference 574426.

Distance: 7 miles (10.5km).

Map: "The Forest of Bowland and Ribblesdale", number 41 in the O.S.
                        "Outdoor Leisure" series.

Public Transport: None except for Summer Sundays and Bank Holidays when the
                        "Bowland Pathfinder" operates a service between Preston and
                        Clitheroe calling at Beacon Fell Country Park.

By car: Leave the M6 at Junction 32 and follow the signs towards Garstang.
                        At the traffic lights in Broughton turn right and follow the signs for
                        Inglewhite and Beacon Fell Country Park.

The Tea Shop

Originally a smithy, the café at Bleasdale is now part of the village Post Office. Its antiquity is revealed in the thick oak beams, pillars and the cream-coloured rendered thick stone walls. Plates, brassware, horse harness and a grandfather clock all help to perpetuate the atmosphere of days long since vanished.

Walkers will appreciate its Afternoon Teas consisting of sandwiches, scones with cream and preserves and home-baked cakes all washed down with copious cups of freshly brewed tea. For those in search of something rather more filling, if that were possible, there is a choice of Sausage and Chips, home-made Steak Pie, Haddock and Chips or Plaice and Chips.

In addition the Bleasdale Cafe offers a whole range of sandwiches, jacket potatoes, soups and salads. There is a selection of fruit pies, depending on the season, and cakes. It makes a more than welcome refreshment stop in a remote and isolated area.

Opening Times: All year, daily, 9am to 5pm. Closed Mondays. **Phone:** 01995 61349.

Beacon Fell

Beacon Fell was designated as a Country Park in 1969, the first in Lancashire and one of the earliest in England. It is an isolated hill top rising to 266 metres (873 feet) located in the Forest of Bowland Area of Outstanding Natural Beauty. It covers 185 acres (112 hectares) of moorland and woodland and is capped by millstone grit.

It takes its name from the warning beacons that were lit on its summit in times of national emergencies such as the approach of the Spanish Armada in 1588. The area is rich in wildlife and there are a number of waymarked trails. A new Visitor Centre was opened in 1995 at Fell House car park, one of several dotted around the park.

Bleasdale

There is no real village centre in Bleasdale. It remains a scattered settlement cradled by a cirque of fells including Parlick, Blindhurst Fell, Fair Snape fell and the Bleasdale Moors.

The name is derived from the Norse word meaning "Light Spot", an apt description which can easily be appreciated by anyone setting foot in the area because of the special quality of the light to be found there. It was originally a part of the Royal Forest of Lancaster.

The parish church of St Eadmer is the only one in this country to bear this dedication. He was a priest of the twelfth century noted for his biographies of St Anselm and other religious figures. Although nominated as Bishop of St Andrews in Scotland, he never occupied his See because of opposition from the Scots. The present church dates only from 1825 but it is known that earlier ones have stood on the same site.

The Bleasdale Circle

This unusual Bronze Age circle was discovered towards the end of the nineteenth century by local farmer Tom Kelsall of Fairsnape Farm. He had noticed that one area of his land was of a different colour to the remainder.

With the assistance of local historian, Leo Shadrach, he excavated

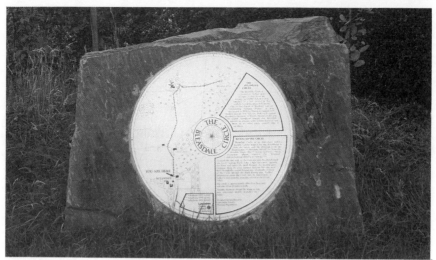

Information on the Bleasdale Circle

the site to discover two circles of wooden posts, one inside the other. At the very centre was a grave containing two burial urns.

These were removed and are now housed in the Harris Museum at Preston. The holes, originally holding the wooden poles, were later filled in with concrete. The Circle which quickly achieved international fame, stands on private ground but permission may be obtained to visit by inquiring at the Bleasdale School, located near St Eadmer's Church, or from the Bleasdale Estate Office at Bleasdale Tower.

The Route

The Post Office at Bleasdale would make an ideal spot for starting this route but the tiny car park is reserved strictly for shop and café customers. It would be unfair on these to leave vehicles parked all day. Roadside parking is not recommended because of the narrow nature of the road. So, instead, it is far better to commence the walk from the Quarry Car Park at Beacon Fell Country Park.

Leave the car park by the entrance and then turn left along the road for approximately ten metres to a junction. Turn right but, after 20 metres and by a footpath sign, make a left turn over a stile and, taking your direction from the arm, head diagonally to the right, skirting to the right of a small depression and descending the sloping field to the bottom right-hand corner and a facing waymarked stile.

Ignore this. Instead turn left along a sunken lane in front of the stile,

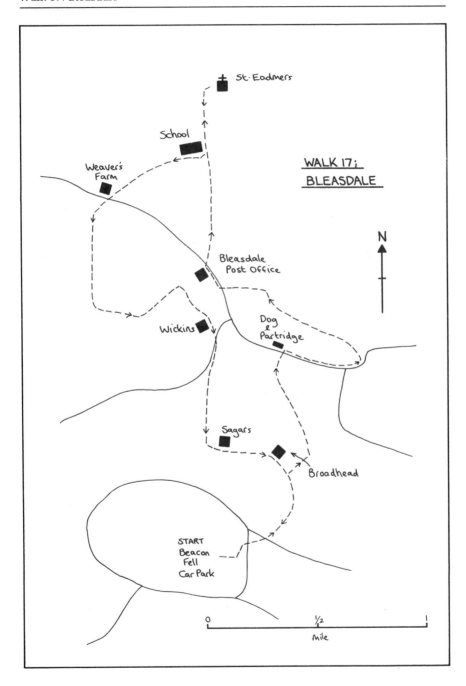

losing altitude gradually to a stile adjacent to a wooden five-barred gate. Longridge Fell is to the right and, beyond that, the great whale-backed hulk of Pendle Hill. Ahead are the Bleasdale Fells.

Negotiate a second stile, this time by a decrepit five-barred gate and ignore another stile on the left. Stay forward for some twenty metres beyond this before turning left over a waymarked stile by yet another metal five-barred gate.

Stay to the right of a hawthorn hedge with Broadhead Farm, screened completely by trees, a short distance to your left. At the next stile stay forward, still walking to the right of a hedge.

In the field corner, and facing King Brow Wood, make a left turn over a stile and then turn sharp right at once. King Brow Wood is now on your right. Veer left down the field to a stile in the left-hand corner.

Over this turn right, as per the waymark, and cross a footbridge before proceeding to the left of a fence. Negotiate another stile, this time in the right-hand corner of the field, and then maintain direction although now to the right of a fence.

On the far side of a facing stile cross another footbridge to emerge onto a minor road facing a white house, formerly the "Dog and Partridge" pub.

Turn right along the road, pass to the left of Bailey Hey Farm and continue a short distance to reach a Z-Bend. On the second angle of this bend make a left turn over an unsigned stone step stile immediately to the right of a metal five-barred gate. Over the stile turn left to walk just to the right of a very well constructed and maintained stone wall.

The turf path provides excellent conditions under foot and the pasture is dotted with enormous patches of nettle. Above, to the right, towers Parlick with its summit reaching 432 metres (1,300 feet) and, further round, is Fair Snape Fell towering to 510 metres (1,550 feet). Completing the cirque are the Bleasdale Fells so creating the impression of walking through a vast, open-air amphitheatre.

Negotiate another stone step stile alongside a wooden five-barred gate and maintain the same general direction to the right of the wall. When the wall is replaced by a stream and fence continue along the distinct path until it curves round towards the right, heading in the direction of a spread of trees.

A short distance before reaching these turn left over a sloping stone clapper bridge to cross a very narrow field to a stile. Immediately cross a wooden footbridge with a stile at the far end and then stay forward to the left of a fence to another stile alongside a footpath sign.

Over this turn right along the road, dropping down the hill for the final 200 metres to reach the café at Bleasdale Post Office.

Suitably refreshed, turn left out of the café to proceed further along the road. Cross a bridge and, a few metres beyond and by a footpath sign, turn right along the surfaced drive leading to Bleasdale School. About 100 metres after the school you will reach St Eadmer's Church.

From the church retrace your steps to the school and, by the far corner, make a right turn onto another surfaced track. By the end of the first field on the left, make a left turn through a wooden, five-barred gate and aim for the corner of the fence ahead. Ignore a stile in the fence and continue forward to the left of it to reach a metal five-barred gate. Pass through into the yard at Weaver's Farm and walk across the centre to gain the road.

Turn right along this but, after a mere five metres, veer left along a narrow, unsigned path which enters some trees. Stay to the right of the fence along the boundary of New Bridge Wood, ignoring two successive stiles on your left before spiralling down briefly to cross a stream and climb a couple of steps.

Follow the clear path with the infant River Brock gurgling along in the same direction although below you to the right. After a stile turn right and lose more height to leave New Bridge Wood and emerge into a lush, green pasture, yet another oasis of peace and quiet.

Head for the wooden footbridge visible directly ahead and, at the far end of this, turn left to pass the foundations of a ruined building before eventually reaching a stile.

Follow the distinct path through the woodlands, initially to the right of a fence and a feeder stream of the Brock. Climb five steps, traverse some marshy ground by means of a line of planks and turn left over the stream by using another wooden footbridge.

At the far end turn right to begin climbing through a shallow clough to reach a stile on the woodland edge. Continue ahead, as directed by the waymark and stay to the right of a row of holly trees and beneath some overhead wires to a stile by an unhinged metal five-barred gate. Ahead, the pear-shaped Parlick is the dominant landscape feature.

Guided by a waymark, maintain the same direction to the right of a fence but, just in front of another five-barred gate, make a left turn over a stile. Ignore this waymark.

Instead, turn right for a distance of 10 metres to a second stile and turn right again, as suggested by another waymark. The ensuing path leads directly to Wicken's Barn, built, as the date indicates, in 1850.

Pass through the small metal gate bearing the blunt message, "Shut Bloody Gate Lad! "

Advance to a double metal gate and reach the road after 15 metres. Turn right along the road. After the second bend and by the footpath sign, make a left turn onto the rough track which leads to Broadhead Farm.

After approximately 1km (half a mile), where the drive to a house called "Heatherway" continues directly ahead, remain along the track as it curves through ninety degrees to the left.

However, within a few metres and before the next wooden five-barred gate, veer-off to the right in accordance with the waymark to pass Sagar's Farm on your left.

Follow the track until making a rendezvous with a junction immediately before reaching Broadhead Farm which is close by on your left. Cross the junction directly to pass through a metal five-barred gate. Proceed a further 10 metres to a waymarker post.

Climb the twisting track to an obvious stile which is located in a gap between two rows of hawthorns. Over this stile make a right turn onto a sunken lane and begin to climb. Negotiate a stile by a five-barred gate and continue upwards for some distance before reaching a waymarked stile on your left.

Ignore this stile. Instead veer diagonally to the right, ascending the steeply sloping field to reach a stile adjacent to a footpath post. Turn right along the road and, at a road junction after 20 metres, turn left for the final few metres to the entrance of the Quarry Car Park on Beacon Fell.

Walk 18: Quernmore

A route along the northern side of the Bowland Fells using field paths, tracks and one stretch of narrow road.

Route: Brow Top – Rowton Brook Farm – Quernmore Village – Terrace Farm – Lower Brow Top – Damas Gill Reservoir – Hare Appletree Farm – Brow Top.

Start: Brow Top Craft Centre, Quernmore. Map reference 528587.

Distance: 5 miles (8km).

Map: "The Forest of Bowland and Ribblesdale", number 41 in the O.S. "Outdoor Leisure" series.

Public Transport: Very occasional buses from Lancaster except on Sundays. On Summer Sundays and Bank Holidays the "Bowland Rambler" bus from Lancaster and Morecambe passes Brow Top.

By car: Leave the M6 at junction 34 and proceed along the A683 to Caton. From there follow the signs to the Trough of Bowland. Brow Top Craft Centre is signed from the centre of Caton. Alternatively from Clitheroe follow the road through Dunsop Bridge and the Trough of Bowland.

The Tea Shop

Opened in 1987, the Brow Top Craft Gallery and Tea Room is housed in a converted barn which carries the date of 1634. So, not surprisingly, it is heavily beamed and has plenty of exposed stonework with the Craft Gallery on the upper floor.

The cakes, all home-made, include Ginger, Eccles, Chorley and Coffee. Cream Teas are a speciality and the scones, laced with ample cream and preserves, are impossible to resist and usually lead to a request for a second.

As usual with many of these Lancashire Tea Rooms located in out-of-the-way places, there is also more filling fare. The great attraction at Brow Top is the Farmhouse Fry-Up which is big enough to sustain you for a walk right across the Bowland Fells – and back again. There is also the usual offering of sandwiches, baked potatoes, soup, beans, chips and eggs not to mention a selection of speciality and herbal teas or freshly-ground coffee.

Opening Times: Summer: Open daily (including Sundays) 11am to 5pm. Winter: Monday to Saturday, 11am to 5pm. Sunday, 12.30pm to 5pm. Closed Wednesdays in Winter. **Phone:** 01524 66833.

Brow Top Tea Room

Brow Top

The Brow Top Craft Centre is run solely for the benefit of local craft workers, providing a retail outlet for their wares. It displays, and sells, the products of some 90 crafts people living within a 25-mile radius of the centre. They include carvings, tapestries, tatting, stained glass, dried flower arrangements, photography and paintings.

At the same time Brow Top remains a working farm covering 20 hectares and bordering open moorland. There is an opportunity of seeing rare breeds of sheep, goats, ponies, rabbits and guinea pigs. There is also a viewfinder in the grounds depicting such famous landmarks as Blackpool Tower, the Lakeland Fells and Heysham Nuclear Power Station on Morecambe Bay.

Quernmore

The name of this scattered upland settlement is derived from the "Querns" or millstones used for grinding corn. These were hewn out of the local rock on nearby Clougha Pike. This, and the moorlands which surround the village, readily explains the origin of the name. A "Saddle Quern" from the area may be seen in the Lancaster Museum.

The early part of this route passes close by the site where, in 1774, excavations revealed the presence of some Roman kilns, complete with pots and other utensils still inside the ovens. These, too, are preserved in the Lancaster Museum. During the eighteenth century a hat-making industry was developed alongside Rooten Brook which is also passed on this walk. The shaggy, stiff woollen hat, using local materials, was once exported for wear by both convicts and slaves.

When Glasson Dock was heavily involved in smuggling many local inhabitants joined in the lucrative trade, as a local poem reveals:

"Once Quernmore lads had other work,
They went on moonlight trips
On pony back with brandy casks,
Discharged from Glasson ships.
If Brandy Barn could only speak
What stories it would tell.
The Yorkshire smugglers cross the Trough
And came here to buy and sell."

In March, 1973, excavations were taking place for a new car park near Jubilee Tower on the moorlands above Quernmore, when two coffins containing the fragments of human hair and toe nails were unearthed. These have been examined by archaeologists who have dated them between 534 and 754 AD. They are displayed in Lancaster Museum.

There is also a strong tradition, neither proved nor disproved, that the whole valley around Quernmore was once a lake. More certainly it became a part of the Royal Forest of Lancaster in 1102 when Roger de Poitou was given Lancaster by the king as a reward for his assistance to William the Conqueror in the invasion of 1066. Timber felled at Quernmore was often used for the carrying out of repairs at Lancaster Castle and also for shipbuilding during times of emergency such as the approach of the Spanish Armada in 1588.

The Route

Leave the car park at Brow Top by walking to the left of the farmhouse and crossing a narrow stream before negotiating a wooden stile in the facing fence. Walk to the left of some pens, followed by a wall while enjoying an extensive view of Morecambe Bay to your left and of the summit of Clougha Pike to your right until you reach a stone step stile in the field corner.

Cross the next field directly to a wooden stile just to the right of Rowton Brook farm. After a further seven metres, negotiate a small wooden gate and swing left, around the house, to a wooden five-barred gate. Through that, follow the farm driveway as it loses altitude rapidly with a swiftly-flowing stream, Rowton Brook, on your left. Descend through a lush, green landscape dotted with isolated field barns and with the site of the former Roman kiln to your right.

After almost a kilometre, cross a cattle grid to meet a road, Quernmore Brow, on a sharp bend by a footpath sign. Turn right and walk around this bend to the cross-roads in the centre of Quernmore village by the Post Office.

Turn left along the road signed to Bay Horse. Beyond "Mardale", a house on the right, embark on a gentle climb but, approximately 250 metres after Terrace Farm, which is on your left, look for the footpath sign to Hare Appletree. By this sign turn left into a lane, soon passing a cottage on your right to reach a stile by a five-barred gate. Continue in the same direction but now climbing more steeply along a footpath to the right of a stone wall. Stay alongside this wall and over a stone step stile until meeting a rough track near a cattle grid and a five-barred gate. Turn right along this track to enjoy another fabulous view, this time out over Glasson Dock, the Lune Estuary and Plover Hill which is close to Cockerham Abbey.

After 100 metres cross a cattle grid and then pass to the right of the house at Lower Brow Top Farm. Proceed to the left of the cattle sheds and continue to the right of a wall, followed by a fence, to a metal five-barred gate. Through this veer slightly to the right while keeping a stream on your left as you cross a large field until coming to the boundary wall of Damas Gill Reservoir.

Continue some 20 metres to the right of this wall until gaining a stone step stile by the end of the embankment. Over this, turn left for the descent onto the clear path which runs below the embankment and heads for the stone house at the far end. The Bowland Fells are both to the right and directly ahead. On reaching the house, pass to the right of the boundary fence to join a track on the far side. Turn right along this, crossing a cattle grid after 100 metres.

There is a babbling brook on your right. Cross a concrete bridge so that the brook flows on your left as the track snakes its way through a shallow valley to cross a second concrete bridge. After this the stream veers away to the moorlands on your right.

At Hare Appletree Farm, walk to the right of the house as the track becomes surfaced. Approximately 200 metres after a dilapidated five-barred gate there is a yellow waymark on your left but it requires an eagle eye to spot it. Make a left turn through the gate by this to walk along a line of hawthorns and then to the left of a fence. The clear, distinct path breasts the brow of the hill before descending to a stile in the right-hand corner of the field. This provides an exit onto a lane.

Turn right along this lane and remain with it until reaching the road which runs through the Trough of Bowland. The entrance to Brow Top Craft Centre is almost opposite.

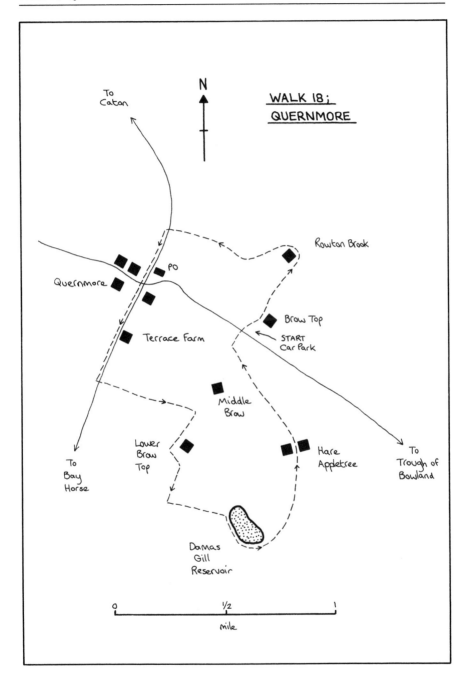

Walk 19: Garstang

An easy, gentle route using towpaths, field paths and tracks through a
mainly pastoral countryside.

Route: Garstang – Th'Owd Tithe Barn – Lancaster Canal – Dimples Bridge –
             Park Head Farm – The Forge – Lingart Lane – River Wyre – Garstang.

Start: Car park by the Tourist Information Centre, Garstang.
             Map reference 494455.

Distance: 6 miles (10km).

Map: "The Forest of Bowland and Ribblesdale", number 41 in the O.S.
             "Outdoor Leisure" series.

Public Transport: Garstang is served by frequent daily buses (including Sundays) from
             Preston, Lancaster, Blackpool and Morecambe.

By car: Garstang is signed from the A6 north of Preston and south of Lancaster.

The Tea Shop

The Court Buttery is to be found in one of the small courtyards off the
main street in the centre of Garstang. Its interior consists of plain white
walls and ceiling with wooden tables and chairs, arranged in the form
of cubicles. In fine weather there are tables and seating outside.

The menu offers a variety of speciality teas and coffees along with
soft drinks and ice cream. There is a selection of scones, cakes and
gateaux while, for those with a larger appetite, there is a substantial
range of plain and toasted sandwiches or dishes such as Lasagne.
Opening Times: Daily, except Sundays, 9.30am to 5.00pm. **Phone:**
01995 602541

Garstang

Garstang owes its importance to its position midway between Preston
and Lancaster where the A6 crosses the River Wyre. This role was
further emphasised with the building of the Lancaster Canal which
flows through the town centre. Today this splendid waterway is used
by pleasure craft and its towpath by walkers.

The Market Cross, erected in the eighteenth century, stands outside
the Royal Oak Hotel and the former Town Hall, a Georgian brick
building, is nearby. The A6 now by-passes the town which retains its
importance as the administrative centre for the Wyre District Council.

The Route

Leave the car park by the main entrance and turn left along High Street. In the Market Place, by the Market Cross and the Royal Oak Hotel, fork right onto Church Street. By the traffic island stay forward into the extension to Church Street, very soon passing the Church of St Thomas on your left. It is notable for its square tower and high nave windows although the interior is of a simple, plain design, the only stained glass being found in the windows behind the altar.

Continue beyond "Th'Owd Tithe Barn", now a pub, which stands on your left. As Church Street becomes Kepple Lane cross the Lancaster Canal by the bridge and, at the far end, turn left to enter a facing track. After about ten metres turn right along the towpath with "Th'Owd Tithe Barn" now on your left on the far side of the canal. Along this stretch of the waterway a number of boats are usually moored.

After some 400 metres cross the Wyre Aqueduct which has a single span of 35 metres. Built by the celebrated Scottish engineer, John Rennie, it was opened to navigation in 1797. To the right at this point is a golf course and Garstang has been left behind to be replaced by a tranquil rural scene.

The Lancaster Canal curves round to the left so offering a distant prospect of the Bowland Fells before passing under Byerworth Bridge. Number 60, this is a graceful arched affair which is followed within 200 metres by the Garstang Turnpike Bridge. This, in turn, is succeeded by bridge number 58, Dimples Bridge, easily recognised by the large green pipes which cross the canal at almost the same spot. Remain with the towpath as it passes beneath Greenhalgh Castyle Bridge, which has no exit, and from where there is a good view of the remains of Greenhalgh castle which is not open to the public.

A few metres before bridge number 56 turn right up a small flight of stone steps to a stile which provides an exit onto a hedged lane. Turn left along this and cross the bridge over the canal to a metal five-barred gate after 100 metres. Negotiate this and, ignoring a stile to the right, stay forward, staying close to the hedge on your left and the field boundary. This path leads to a choice of stiles: a traditional wooden one or one of the stone step variety. Both are waymarked and are located in the field corner close to a pylon.

Having selected your preference, continue forward, still to the right of a hedge, passing beneath overhead wires to another stile. Beyond this proceed to the right of an oak woodland and a wooden footpath post, maintaining the same line of direction towards the main railway line from London to Glasgow and the M6 Motorway which run alongside each other at this point.

Beyond the footpath post gradually swing round to the left whilst drawing closer and closer to the railway and aiming for an obvious footpath finger post standing on the right-hand boundary of the field. By this footpath post turn right over a stile onto a bridge spanning a disused railway. At the far end of the bridge turn left over a stile to follow the path down the embankment onto the former track of the abandoned railway. **Note:** do not cross either the main west coast railway line or the M6 motorway at this point.

At the foot of the embankment turn right along the former railway as it passes through an embankment. This is a concessionary footpath through the newly created Wildgoose Wood Nature Reserve. In Summer, meadow brown butterflies are to be seen as they flit from gorse to harebells and foxgloves.

After several hundred metres, negotiate a stile in the fence which crosses the track and immediately turn right to climb up the embankment to a waymarked stile. Over this veer diagonally to the right as directed, gradually moving away from the fence towards the far corner of Castle Wood and a very tall ladder stile which provides access to a lane. Turn right along this to cross both the main railway line and the M6 before reaching Park Head Farm which bears the date of 1730. By the far corner of the farm turn left over a small concrete bridge to pass at once to the right of a small barn to meet a metal five-barred gate.

Through this advance some 25 metres to the left of a hedge, pass through a gap in a facing hedge and proceed to the right of the motorway fence. New Hall farm is away to your right. Turn left over a ladder stile in the field corner and then turn right, walking within centimetres of the Motorway hard shoulder but separated from it by a fence. The traffic is hurtling past at 90 m.p.h.

Cross a culverted stream which may be observed cascading down a flight of steps on your right. Within 15 metres turn right over a ladder stile before veering right and staying to the left of a hedge to another stile, this time adjacent to a wooden five-barred gate and providing an exit onto a narrow surfaced road, Keeper's Road. Turn left to re-cross the M6 motorway and the London to Glasgow Railway with a splendid view of the Bleasdale Fells some distance to your right.

By "Forge Cottage", a white house standing close to the ruins of a former forge, the road bends to the right with an old-fashioned gypsy caravan (see overleaf) located in a small paddock on the right. 250 metres beyond "Forge Cottage" the road bends again, this time to the left and passes Higher Lingart Farm. A few metres beyond the Farm, leave the road where it bends sharply to the right and maintain direction into the hedged Lingart Lane, passing beneath two sets of overhead wires in quick succession.

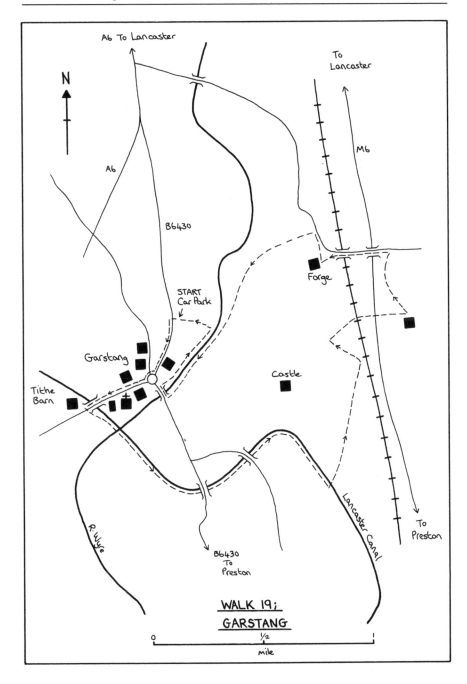

Gypsy caravan at Forge Cottage, Garstang

A hundred metres after the entrance to Lower Lingart Farm turn left over a stile in the hedge and then stay to the left of another hedge forming the field boundary. Where this hedge corners away to the right, remain forward on the distinct path to a waymarked stile. In crossing the next field veer left, taking your general direction from the clearly visible tower of the Catholic church in the hamlet of Bonds.

The well-used path reaches a stile. Cross the centre of the ensuing field to another stile and then veer right, as shown by the waymark, to cross a surfaced road. Ten metres beyond, turn left over another stile so that the River Wyre is on your right as it tumbles over a weir.

Remain to the left of the river and, where it curves away to form a loop on your right, maintain direction to a waymarked stile. Continue forward along the base of a small slope on your left until reaching another waymarker post. By this, go left, once again along the banks of the Wyre, to reach a stile. Cross the following field to its far left-hand corner where a wooden footbridge leads immediately to Bonds Lane.

Turn right for two metres to meet the B6430. At this junction make another right turn to cross Garstang Bridge spanning the Wyre. Where the road branches, fork right into Bridge Street and, after approximately 50 metres, turn right into the signed Riverside Path. Surfaced, this carries you back to your starting point in the car park by the Tourist Information Centre.

Walk 20: Scorton

A walk which commences by ascending to the summit of Nicky Nook before descending into Grize Dale and following the shores of the reservoir.

Route: Scorton – Snowhill Lane – Wyresdale Park – Nicky Nook – Grize Dale – Higher Lane – Tithe Barn Lane – Scorton.

Start: Scorton village centre. Map reference 503487.

Distance: 4 miles (6.5km).

Map: "The Forest of Bowland and Ribblesdale", number 41 in the O.S. "Outdoor Leisure" series.

Public Transport: Occasional buses from Garstang. Phone: 01524 841656.

By car: Scorton is reached by minor roads signed from the A6 in Cabus, north of Garstang. There is no car park but limited roadside parking is possible in the village.

The Tea Shop

Set snugly off the main road through the village, the Priory Tea Rooms are almost submerged with creeping plants. The beamed interior, with its white walls enlivened by displays of plates and prints, offers an inviting atmosphere. The wooden tables, covered with white and burgundy tablecloths, provide that aura of luxury and elegance which is completed by the floral curtains. In fine weather there are tables outside.

The menu is all-embracing starting with an All-Day Breakfast and including a Two-Course Lunch. There is a complete A la Carte selection. Smaller appetites are catered for with salads, sandwiches and Lite-Bites.

For that mid afternoon break there are Cream Teas, Afternoon Teas, scones and an amazingly wide choice of cakes and gateaux, all home-made and designed to tempt you to abandon all ideas of slimming. Any or all these may be accompanied by a choice of speciality teas or coffees, hot chocolate with cream, or soft drinks and milk shakes. It is certainly not a tea shop for the faint-hearted but a Mecca for the lovers of cream.

Scorton

Scorton is a pretty village with its stone cottages clustered around the

The Priory, Scorton

centre and the entrance to Wyresdale Park. Its parish church, set on raised ground at the southern end of the village, has an imposing spire which is a familiar landmark to all who travel the M6 Motorway.

The Route

Starting from the Post Office cross the main road directly into Snowhill Lane, soon passing the War Memorial, the Old School House dated 1861 and the Catholic Church of St Mary and St James, all on your left. Initially the climb is steep but the gradient eases as the lane crosses the M6 Motorway by a bridge and passes the boundary stone of the Bowland Area of Outstanding Natural Beauty.

Although surfaced, Snowhill Lane carries little traffic and is lined with foxglove, wild roses, red campion and ragged robin while sheep graze the pastures on either side.

By the entrance to Wyresdale Park the lane bends sharply to the right, passes through trees and crosses a small stone bridge before resuming its steep limb to reach a T-junction at the foot of the bracken-covered fell side.

Stay forward to cross the narrow road directly to a wooden kissing gate adjacent to a footpath sign which reads, "Public Footpath to Nicky Nook for Grize Dale Valley, 1 mile."

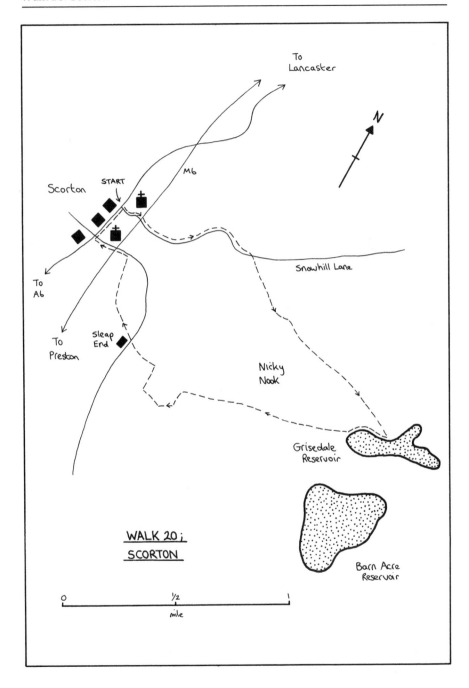

To
Lancaster

N

Scorton   START   Mb

To
A6

To
Preston   Sleap
End

Snowhill Lane

Nicky
Nook

Grisedale
Reservoir

WALK 20;
SCORTON

Barn Acre
Reservoir

0   ½   1
                   mile

Through the gate climb a short flight of steps to follow the well worn footpath as it climbs steeply up the fell while passing through gorse and bracken. Behind the view gradually opens-up to reveal the whole stretch of Morecambe Bay, Heysham Nuclear Power Station, Lancaster University and the coastal plain.

Where the gradient eases slightly pass to the left of a low embankment topped by a wire fence which encloses a tiny reservoir. Continue to the right of another fence and a derelict stone wall to reach a footpath sign and waymarker on your left.

After a further fifteen metres negotiate another waymarked wooden kissing gate and then continue along the same line of direction, although somewhat less steeply, with a wall on your left. This excellent path traverses the open moorland where the occasional tree has been sculpted by the prevailing westerly wind.

After passing to the left of the end of a stone wall, veer to the right across more open moorland while gradually moving further and further away from a small tarn and a new plantation which are a short distance to your left. The path is still ascending but more gradually as it eventually curves to the left and rounds a cairn of stones before arriving at the Triangulation Pillar on the summit of Nicky Nook at a height of 215 metres.

Ahead is a broad sweep of the Bowland Fells while to the right Barnacres and Grizedale Lea Reservoirs are clearly visible and so, too, are the radio masts above Oakenclough.

From the Triangulation Pillar continue forward on the clearly defined path as it loses altitude slightly whilst heading for an obvious ladder stile over a facing wall. This provides excellent upland walking that is easy on the feet.

Do not negotiate the ladder stile. Instead, as directed by the notice, turn right and, keeping the wall on your left, follow the path as it bends round to the left and loses height rapidly through a sea of bracken to pass a waymarker post and a seat dedicated to Mark Damian Lavelle "a keen mountaineer and fell walker" who died in 1993 aged 31.

Some caution is required here because there are loose stones on the path which is extremely steep. Down below on your right Grize Dale Reservoir almost invariably attracts a few screaming oyster-catchers.

Eventually the path drops to a stone step stile which provides access onto a bridleway by a 3-armed footpath post. Turn right along the Grize Dale Valley with the reservoir on your immediate left.

In its higher reaches the valley is narrow and steep-sided. Pass through a wooden kissing gate adjacent to a wooden five-barred one and, at a junction some 50 metres beyond and recognisable by a waymark, fork left with the main bridleway while continuing to lose height.

After more than a kilometre negotiate a metal five-barred gate by a 4-armed footpath post. Immediately turn right, leaving the bridleway to use a path signed to Higher Lane. By the wood swing left up the slope and keep a fence on your right until reaching a small wooden gate by another footpath sign.

Through this gate turn right along Higher Lane which is surfaced.

Climb slightly to pass Sleap End and, a few yards beyond, climb over the stile in the hedge on your left. Then veer to the right, heading downhill to pass through a gateway in the right-hand field corner. Continue along the same line of direction to pass to the right of an electricity sub-station in the corner of the next field. There negotiate a metal five-barred gate to emerge onto Tithe Barn Lane.

Turn left, pass beneath the M6 Motorway and continue as far as the junction with Gubberford Lane. Turn right, pass to the left of the church and walk the few remaining metres into the centre of Scorton village.

Walk 21: Knott End

Using mainly tracks and lanes, this route follows the Wyre Estuary with its extensive mudflats before swinging inland to cross extremely fertile farmland.

Route: Knott End – Canshe Bank – Hackensall Hall – Barnaby's Sands – Coat Walls Farm – Curwen's Hill – Knott End.

Start: Car Park, Quail Holm Road, Knott End. Map reference 347484.

Distance: 5 miles (8km).

Map: "Fleetwood", number 658 in the O.S. "Pathfinder" series.

Public Transport: Knott End is served by frequent daily buses from Blackpool, Lancaster (not Sundays) and Garstang (not Sundays).

By car: From the M6 take the M 55 and leave at Junction 3 (Corner Row). Follow the A585 to Skippool and turn right onto the A588 across Shard Bridge. Just beyond Stalmine fork left onto the B5377 which leads into Knott End.

The Tea Shop

The Knott End Cafe is a spacious modern building overlooking the ferry landing stage. Through its large picture windows it commands some outstanding views of the Wyre Estuary and out across the vast stretch of Morecambe Bay.

The excellence of the views is matched by the extensive menu which ranges from a simple cup of tea to more substantial fare including, as befits a seaside village, Breaded Haddock, Battered Cod and Scampi. There is Cottage Pie, Shepherd's Pie, Steak and Kidney Pie, omelettes with various fillings and a wide choice of sandwiches.

To complete any meal or simply accompany that pot of freshly-brewed tea there is a bewildering array of fruits pies, their contents governed by the seasons, and gateaux including lemon Meringue and Chocolate Fudge Cake, all served with generous portions of cream or ice-cream. Of course, for something a little plainer, there is always a scone with preserves and cream. Whatever the choice, they are all home-made.

Opening Times: All year Mondays to Saturdays 10am to 6pm. Sundays 9am to 6pm. **Phone:** 01253 811948.

Wyre Estuary and Fleetwood from Knott End

Knott End

Knott End is really nothing more than a pleasant coastal village situated at the mouth of the Wyre, a river which rises on the Bowland Fells and flows through Garstang before reaching the sea on Morecambe Bay. There are no amusement arcades or fun rides but a market on Sundays all year round and also on Wednesdays between July and September. It enjoys an excellent selection of shops in the village centre.

Knott End is probably best known, however, for the small passenger ferry which links it directly with Fleetwood across the mouth of the Wyre. It operates during the summer months only and is very dependent on the tides.

The Route

Exit the car park by turning left into Quaile Holme Road and, after about twenty metres, making another left turn into Bourne May Road. Turn left again to pass in front of the Knott End Cafe and to reach a wooden footpath finger post by the sea after a distance of some 20 metres.

On a clear day this spot provides a wide-ranging view out over Morecambe Bay which embraces the nuclear power station at Heysham as well as the more distant Lake District hills. Directly ahead, across the very mouth of the River Wyre, stands Fleetwood, often with an Isle of Man Ferry and other ocean-going vessels tied-up in the docks.

By the finger post turn left yet again to follow the path along Canshe Bank which is the first section of the Wyre Way, a 16-mile route around the estuary to Fleetwood. Pass the Coastguard Station on your left with Fleetwood Docks across the river to your right. The path follows the course of the river as it snakes its passage through the extensive mudflats at low tide and a golf course materialises on your left.

After approximately half a kilometre, and directly in front of the white Sea Dyke Cottage, built in 1754, turn left to follow the path signed to Hackensall. At the subsequent T-junction, reached after a mere fifty metres, make a right turn onto a wide chatter track over the golf course.

After 40 metres, and by a group of sheds, veer leftwards along the golf course boundary with a fence on your right. By one of the holes and a tee, the track acquires a surface for a few metres. Where this surface terminates, with a white cottage down below on your right, swing through 45 degrees to the left as directed by a footpath sign.

Cross the golf course while aiming a shade to the left of another collection of sheds and a wooden electricity pylon. By these the path develops into a track which quickly reaches a T-junction by the deserted Hackensall Farm. Turn left so that the farm is on your right. Just beyond the farm, the track passes between gateposts and turns sharply to the left along Whinny Lane to meet a two-armed finger post after 100 metres.

By this turn right to follow another broad track, this time signed as part of the Wyre Way to Barnaby's Sands.

Initially this passes through trees but, after 25 metres, crosses a blocked cattle grid to enter more open countryside. The slope on the right rises to a magnificent 15 metres above sea level, while another section of the golf course in on your left.

The track twists and turns for well in excess of a kilometre until, having passed beneath two sets of overhead wires within ten metres of each other, it arrives at a junction with another two-armed finger post. This is Barnaby's Sands, a stretch of the river notorious for its dangerous mudflats which attract large flocks of wading birds during the winter months. Twenty metres beyond the signpost a stile facilitates entrance to the nature reserve run by the Lancashire Wildlife Trust.

However, instead of advancing to this, turn left by the footpath post to walk another broad track signed to Town End. The overhead wires now run parallel.

After some 600 metres follow the track around to the left, as directed by two sets of waymarks, so heading directly towards Coat Walls Farm

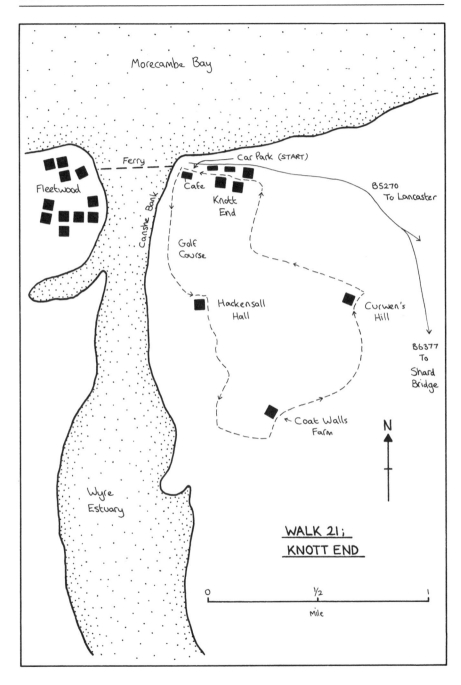

Morecambe Bay

Ferry

Fleetwood

Canshe Bank

Car Park (START)

Cafe

Knott End

B5270 To Lancaster

Golf Course

Hackensall Hall

Curwen's Hill

B6377 To Shard Bridge

Coat Walls Farm

N

Wyre Estuary

WALK 21; KNOTT END

0   ½   1

mile

which often flies the Union Jack. Pass under the overhead wires and, immediately in front of the farm with its white house and outbuildings, turn sharply to the right so remaining with the track.

Cross a cattle grid with a stile alongside and pass a small pond on the right before reaching another cattle grid and a T-junction with a foot-path finger post. Turn left towards Curwen's Hill Farm for a steady but gentle climb for approximately half a kilometre.

On reaching Curwen's Hill Farm pass between the house, dated 1735, and the outbuildings to negotiate a stile. Stay forward along an obscure path which runs immediately to the right of a fence as it descends a small bank to a metal kissing gate in the field corner. This provides entry onto a traditional hedged lane.

Turn left along this and, ignoring all side paths and tracks, maintain direction until the lane bends sharply to the right before passing between two houses to gain the end of Hackensall Road.

Turn right and, after approximately 1km, turn left into Quaile Holme Road which leads directly back to your starting point.

Walk 22: Glasson Dock

A route which offers fine views of the southern section of Morecambe Bay as it crosses drained flats and follows the sea wall.

Route: Glasson Dock – Tithe Barn Hill – Marsh Lane – Crook Farm – Cockersand Abbey – Gardener's Farm – Kendal Hill – Old Glasson – Glasson Dock.

Start: Car park, Glasson Dock. Map reference 445562.

Distance: 6 miles (9.5km).

Map: "Galgate and Dolphinholme", number 659 in the O.S. "Pathfinder" series.

Public Transport: There are several buses daily to Glasson Dock from Lancaster. No Sunday service.

By car: Take the B5290 from Conder Bridge which is located on the A588 a few miles south of Lancaster.

The Tea Shop

The "Light O'er the Lune" café is a modern, functional brick building commanding excellent views out over the marina and the working dock. These provide a temptation to linger, watching the contrasting maritime activities. It has formica-panelled walls with tables to match and it is a case of counter service.

The menu is as extensive as Morecambe Bay, with a strong emphasis on seafood with freshly caught Haddock, Cod, Plaice and Scampi on offer. Lune Salmon is a speciality of the house. These are complemented by All-Day Breakfasts, burgers and a variety of meat pies, including Steak and Kidney. For anyone anxious to sample something rather less substantial the café offers any number of fruit pies, ice creams and cakes, including Bakewell Tarts and Chorley Cakes.

Opening Times: All year: Monday to Friday, 10am to 5.30pm. Saturdays, 10am to 6pm. Sundays, 9am to 6pm. **Phone:** 01534 751489

Glasson Dock

As the passage into Lancaster Docks became more difficult because of the silting-up of the Lune and the increasing size of merchant ships, Glasson Docks was conceived as the official Port of Lancaster to which

The Anchor, Glasson Dock

it was linked by an arm of the Lancaster Canal. Its success was short-lived although even today it remains as a working port, principally concerned with coastal traffic. It also boasts a large marina for pleasure craft.

Cockersand Abbey

Apart from the stone remnants of a few walls, little remains of Cocker-sand Abbey other than a rather impressive Chapter House. This has survived intact because it was adapted for use as a mausoleum or burial place for members of the Dalton Family of nearby Thurnham Hall.

This bleak and isolated spot on the Lune Estuary appears to have been adopted first by a hermit named Hugh who established a monastic cell in pre-Norman times. He attracted a number of pilgrims but following the Norman Conquest of 1066 it was used as a leper hospital. It was not until 1190 that the monks of the Premonstratensian Order founded an abbey on the site. It was called St Mary's of the Marsh and quickly grew to be one of the wealthiest in the county.

In common with all other such establishments it was dissolved by Henry VII1 at the Reformation and much of the stonework, a very valuable commodity in these parts, was used in the building of local farmhouses and sea defence works.

The monks were responsible for the construction of the first light-house along this particular stretch of coastline. The present lighthouse, still visible on Plover Scar off Plover Hill, was erected in 1840 to guide shipping on its way to Lancaster into the navigation channel of the River Lune.

The Route

Leave by the car park entrance and turn left. After a few metres, by a large anchor and opposite to the Victoria Inn, make another left turn to cross the swing bridge which separates the marina from the dock. Proceed in the same direction to pass to the left of the "Light O'er the Lune" café and then the Post Office before embarking on the steep climb up Tithe Barn Hill.

On gaining the crest at 20 metres above sea level it is worth pausing for a few moments to use the special viewfinder which indicates the various features of interest in its 180 degrees sweep. By sitting on one of the bench seats provided it is possible to spend a few extra minutes admiring the view across Morecambe Bay which embraces Heysham Nuclear Power Station, the Isle of Man, the Lake District Fells, the white-domed folly in Williamson Park, the Italianate architecture of Lancaster University, Sunderland Point and the sweep of the Bowland Fells.

At this junction of Tithe Barn Hill with Bodie Hill turn left along the road which is signed as a stretch of the Lancashire Coastal Way. After half a kilometre, as the road begins to lose height while bending acutely to the left, turn right into Marsh Lane, also part of the Coastal Way.

Pass a caravan park on your left and continue through a wooden five-barred gate. Where the flanking hedgerows terminate, stay forward to the left of the occasional hawthorn to traverse the drained marshland where cattle graze. The broad track is clear and easy to follow as it negotiates a second five-barred gate by the wide drainage channel known as Janson Pool and then proceeds over the marshland to reach the coast just to the left of Crook Farm where another decorative anchor is featured.

By the footpath finger post turn left along the embankment walking to the left of the sea and the bird reserve which is the winter haunt of thousands of wading birds. Because of the dangerous nature of the quicksands do not venture onto the foreshore.

Using the sea wall pass Crook Cottage and the strangely-shaped Abbey Lighthouse Cottage. 250 metres beyond this negotiate a kissing gate and continue with the broad sweep of the coast around Plover Hill with Knott End and Fleetwood visible in the far distance. Plover Light is on your right. This section of the route is a forlorn spot at low tide.

Pass through the next kissing gate and then swing leftwards across the field towards the ruins of Cockersand Abbey. Follow the clear path over the greensward as it passes to the right of the Chapter House before it curves further left to a stile by the deserted farmhouse of Cockersand Abbey Farm.

Keep to the left of the house, corner it and continue until reaching a barn. By this turn left through a waymarked five-barred gate before following the wide track to a stile by another five-barred gate and reaching a road.

Turn left along this road and, at the subsequent Y-junction with Slack Lane, fork right into Moss Lane. Ignore all footpath signs until reaching Gardner's Farm. By the far corner of this, and by a footpath sign, go over the stile on your left and then pass an electricity sub-station on your right before meeting a wooden five-barred gate.

Cross the middle of the next field to a metal five-barred gate and maintain direction to the right of a ditch and hedge to yet another five-barred gate. Guided by the clear path reach Kendal Hill Farm.

There turn right through a green five-barred gate but, after a further seven metres, turn left over a strange stile, part stone and part metal set into the wire fence. Stay to the right of a fence and red brick bungalow while heading for another five-barred gate in the left-hand corner of the field. Negotiate this and make a left turn through yet another to emerge onto Dobbs Lane.

Turn right along this hedged lane, passing Old Glasson Farm before meeting your outward route on Tithe Barn Lane and retracing your steps.

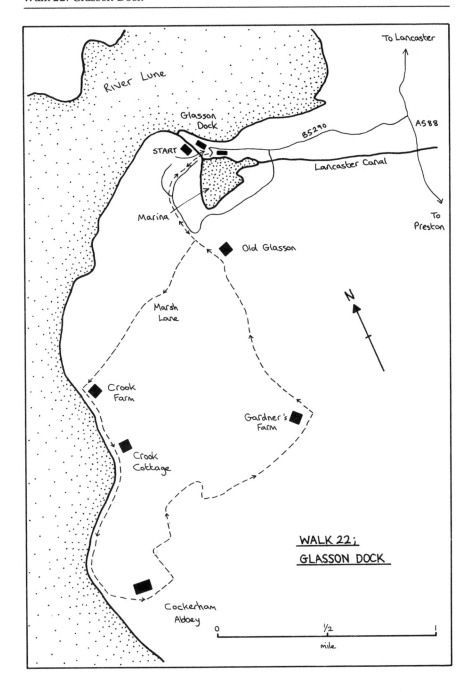

To Lancaster

River Lune

Glasson Dock

B5290

A588

START

Lancaster Canal

To Preston

Marina

Old Glasson

Marsh Lane

N

Crook Farm

Gardner's Farm

Crook Cottage

WALK 22; GLASSON DOCK

Cockerham Abbey

0   1/2   1
mile

Walk 23: Galgate

A short walk using mainly field paths and canal towpath on a circular route
to the south of Lancaster.

Route: Galgate Craft Centre – Galgate – Hampson's Lane – Lancaster Canal
                    – Junction Bridge – Galgate Craft Centre.

Start: Canalside Craft Centre, Galgate. Map reference 484551.

Distance: 2½ miles (4km).

Map: "The Forest of Bowland and Ribblesdale", number 41 in the O.S.
                    "Outdoor Leisure" series.

Public Transport: Frequent daily (including Sunday) buses to Galgate from Lancaster,
                    Morecambe, Garstang and Preston.

By car: Galgate is on the A6 a few miles south of Lancaster. Leave the M6
                    Motorway at Junction 33 and travel one mile north. There is a car park
                    at the craft centre.

The Tea Shop

The Tea Rooms at the Canalside Craft Centre in Galgate are housed in
a converted barn complete with wooden beams and rendered white
walls. Its pine tables are partnered by spindle-backed chairs. It offers a
wide menu including toasted teacakes, soup, toasted sandwiches,
baked jacket potatoes with a choice of filling, Cheese and Onion Pie,
Cottage Pie and Lasagne, not to mention its Mushroom and Nut Fet-
tucini. There is a wonderful offering of home-baked, mouth-watering
cakes including Lemon, Chocolate and Flake. Coffee, tea and soft drinks
are also available.

Opening Times: Daily all year except Monday, 10am to 5pm. **Phone:**
01524 752223.

Galgate

Galgate was once renowned for its silk mills, some of which may still
be seen along the main road of the village. It was also an important
staging post on the old turnpike road between Lancaster and Preston.
Its importance was enhanced by its position on the Lancaster Canal as
it stood close to the Glasson Dock junction. In former times it had a busy

Galgate Marina, Lancaster Canal

quay where cargoes were loaded and unloaded. This has been replaced by a flourishing marina for pleasure boats.

The Route

From the Canalside Craft Centre turn left along the busy A6, passing under the railway arch before reaching the traffic lights in the centre of the village. Turn right along the road signed to Quernmore, soon climbing beyond Launds Field caravan site on your right. Twenty metres beyond Vale House, climb over the metal ladder stile with bow-shaped handles on your right.

Advance to a wooden footbridge. From the far end climb the sloping field while steering a course slightly to the right of two oak trees. On reaching the facing fence swing right to walk with it on your left until reaching a stile on the crest of the hill. Turn left over this before veering slightly towards the left while losing height to the next stile.

Maintain the same general direction towards the fence bordering the M6 Motorway slip road. On finding further progress barred by this, turn right along the field boundary. In the corner make a left turn over a stile and descend a flight of concrete steps. At the bottom turn left and pass beneath the road bridge with the London to Glasgow main West Coast railway line on your immediate right.

At the far end make another left turn, this time climbing a flight of four steps before making a right turn over a stile and then staying to the left of a fence to a ladder stile by a footpath post which provides an exit onto Hampson Lane.

Turn right and walk over the railway bridge to reach the A6 within a hundred metres.

Using the central reservation, cross the A6 and turn right. Stay to the left of the traffic island but, just by the northern end of it, make a left turn onto an unsigned lane to meet a metal five-barred gate after five metres.

Climb the partially overgrown hedged lane to a stile and then stay forward a little to the right of a fence. Corner the field, remaining alongside the hedge-cum-fence. Follow it round when it turns fairly sharply to the left and leads to a double-arched bridge spanning the Lancaster Canal.

At the far end is a stile. Negotiate this and turn right to walk immediately to the left of a fence until reaching another stile in a field corner. This provides access onto the towpath of the Lancaster Canal at the point where the Glasson Dock branch leaves the main waterway. Cross the steeply arched and cobbled bow bridge to gain the towpath of the main canal.

Follow the sign pointing towards Lancaster and remain along the towpath for approximately one kilometre until meeting the first bridge.

Immediately before this negotiate the small gate on the left and advance for five metres to meet a wide track. Turn right, cross the Galgate Bridge and return to the Canalside Craft Centre which is on your left.

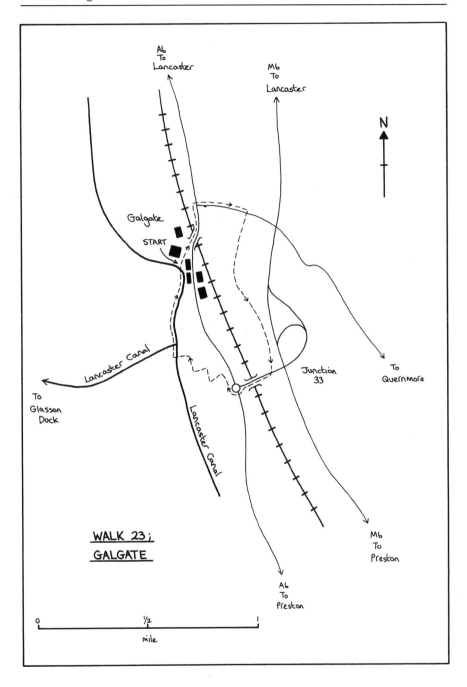

A6
To
Lancaster

M6
To
Lancaster

N

Galgate

START

Lancaster Canal

To
Glasson
Dock

Lancaster Canal

Junction
33

To
Quernmore

WALK 23;
GALGATE

M6
To
Preston

A6
To
Preston

0   ½   1
mile

Walk 24: Caton

An easy, gentle route following riverside paths and returning via a disused railway line converted into a walking trail.

Route: Crook o' Lune – Arkle Beck – Waterworks Bridge – Ellers Farm – Caton – Crook o' Lune.

Start: Crook o' Lune car park and picnic site. Map reference 522647.

Distance: 4 miles (6.5km)

Map: "Forest of Bowland and Ribblesdale", number 41 in the O.S. "Outdoor Leisure" series.

Public Transport: Caton is served by frequent daily (including Sundays) buses from Lancaster, Kirkby Lonsdale and Ingleton. There is also a daily service from Leeds, including Sundays).

By car: The Crook o' Lune car park and picnic area are signed from the A683 just before entering the village of Caton from Lancaster. If travelling along the M6 Motorway leave at Junction 34 and follow the signs to Kirkby Lonsdale.

The Tea Shop

With its brilliant white frontage and central location on the A683 in the middle of Caton village, "The Cottage Tea Room" is impossible to miss. The antiquity of the building is confirmed by the date of 1695 carved over the front entrance and, in keeping with this, the thick, wooden beams of the interior still carry the original adze marks.

The deep-set windows are housed in thick stone walls and are partnered by two enormous fireplaces with stone surrounds. The walls are decorated with a selection of pictures and water colours, many of which are for sale. A genuinely cosy atmosphere is created by the floral table cloths and carpets.

Lisa Malloch, who assumed responsibility for managing "The Cottage Tea Room" in the summer of 1996, offers freshly baked baguettes with a range of unusual fillings from Poached Salmon to Strips of Sirloin Accompanied by Onion Rings and also including Hand-Carved Ham and Warmed Brie with Bacon. Her melting sandwiches may tempt you with their fillings of Stilton garnished with Bacon and Mushrooms or Lancashire Cheese with Onion. Similar fillings are available in baked potatoes. Main courses include Poached Salmon with creamy Dill

Cottage Tea Room

Sauce, Lamb Cutlets marinaded with Balsamic Vinegar and Rosemary, home-made Steak and Kidney Pie and Beer-Battered Haddock.

For the afternoon walker there is a selection of home-made cakes second-to-none including scones with jam and cream, Danish Pastries, Millionaire's Shortbread, Squidgy Chocolate Cake, Lemon Cake, Walnut Cake and Carrot Cake. The choice of teas includes Lancaster Blend, Assam, Earl Grey or Darjeeling. There is also a selection of coffees and soft drinks. **Opening Times: All** year: Monday closed. Tuesday 12 noon to 8pm. Wednesday to Saturday 11am to 9pm. Sunday 12 to 8pm.

Caton

Originally the village was centred around the Norman Church of St Paul with its cluster of houses but the heart of the village moved to its present site with the construction of the Lancaster to Richmond Turnpike in the eighteenth century and also with the arrival of cotton mills which used the fast flowing waters of Arkle and Forge Becks. The name, Caton, is of Norse origin and the village was once noted for its "Fish Stones". Located in Arkle Beck, these were joined by metal ties and it was from them that the monks from Cockersand Abbey sold the salmon netted in the Lune Estuary which was surplus to their requirements.

Caton Low Mill still stands and is near the route of this walk.

Constructed in 1783 by Thomas and John Hodgson, it was powered by a water wheel. In 1814 it was taken over by the Gregg Family who were the noted owners of Styal Mill in Cheshire. They remained in control until the Cotton Famine created by the American Civil War, 1861 to 1865. The mill survived this disaster to continue in operation until the 1970s when it finally closed. It achieved the distinction of being the mill to have the longest continuous production record in Lancashire.

Lancaster-Wennington Railway

Originally known as the "Little North Western" to distinguish it from the genuine article, this strange railway line was opened in 1849. It was an economic disaster from the outset. On the day it was scheduled to open it had no rolling stock and the improvised carriages eventually used were of such a design that, if left open, they swept everything from the platforms. In 1852 it was absorbed by the Midland Railway, becoming a part of the LMS in 1923. Forty years later it fell victim to Dr. Beeching's Axe and was taken over by Lancashire County Council for conversion into a walking trail.

The Crook o' Lune

This famous beauty spot with its well-wooded slopes is located just to the west of Caton. The winding course of the River Lune was formed towards the end of the Ice Ages as the river cut a winding channel through the high ground. It was a favourite spot of the poet Wordsworth who recommended everyone to travel north by way of the Crook o' Lune simply to enjoy the views. In 1816 these views were captured on canvas by the landscape painter Turner.

The Route

Leave the Crook o'Lune car park by the path near the entrance which is signed to the picnic area. Descend the short slope for some 20 metres to a three-fingered footpath sign adjacent to the former railway line. Turn left over the green metal bridge which once carried the railway over the Lune and is signed in the direction of Caton.

At the far end of this bridge and by a Lancashire County Council display panel, turn right down a flight of steps signed to the picnic area. At the foot of these steps negotiate the stile and then turn to the right down a very short slope towards the river. Turn right again to pass under the bridge following the clear path with the Lune on your left.

The walking is excellent: the turf under foot is soft and springy, the flat-bottomed valley is lush and the flanking, rolling hills dotted with sheep. Your approach will probably flush groups of mallard from the wide, steady-flowing river at this point.

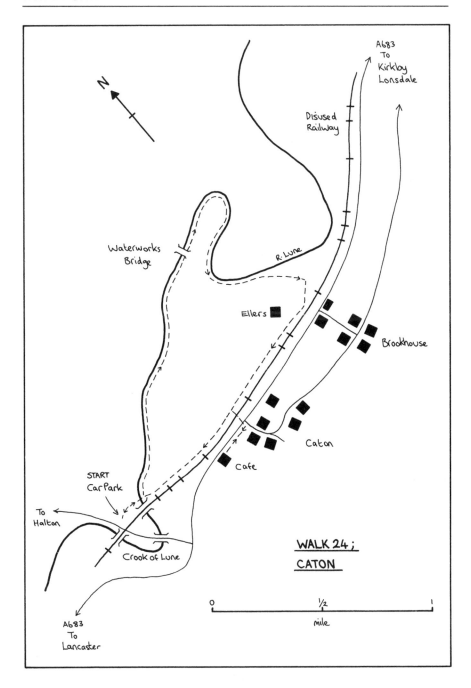

WALK 24;
CATON

Pass beneath some overhead wires and continue forwards over a stile adjacent to a five-barred gate which is almost invariably open. Negotiate another stile and maintain the same direction to pass a weir. Stay to the right of a square, stone tower owned by the National Rivers Authority and, later, of a small wooden hut. The path eventually reaches the banks of Arkle Beck, just a few metres from its confluence with the Lune.

Cross the stepping stones and maintain direction to the right of the Lune to another stile and then the Waterworks Bridge, a metal structure on stone piers. Immediately beyond this, keep left of a line of ancient boundary stones to regain the river bank before reaching yet another stile. Over this, the path clings to the Lune as it curves through a very acute bend to the right. In effect you double back on yourself to walk in the opposite direction while still remaining to the right of the river.

Shortly after negotiating another stile by some willow trees, swing left to a stile by a five-barred gate. Continue forwards still alongside the river, to yet another stile located some 5 metres to the left of a five-barred gate. Through this maintain direction to pass a metal compound on your right to a stile by a double five-barred gate.

This provides an entry into a lane. Go forward some 20 metres along this and then turn right, still following the lane and ignoring a way-marked stile on your left. Instead, bend left with the lane as directed by a yellow waymarker fixed to a fence. After approximately 250 metres it swings through ninety degrees to the right. Cross a stile by a five-barred gate with Ellers Farm a short distance away on your right.

After a further 250 metres, pass a house on your right and, 100 metres further and within a few metres of the A683, make a right turn through a small wooden gate to join the walking trail along the line of the former Lancaster to Wennington Railway. Cross Arkle Beck once again, this time by a bridge, and, after a further ten metres, negotiate a small wooden gate. The houses of Caton are now close-by on your left.

Continue along the trail until reaching a footpath sign alongside a five-barred gate and wooden barrier. At this point turn right through a small wooden gate and then sharp left along a narrow road with the black and white "Station House" on your right.

Continue for 100 metres to meet the A683 by Barclay's Bank. Turn right along the pavement for 200 metres to reach the "Cottage Tea Room". Suitably refreshed, retrace your steps as far as the "Station House" and then make a left turn by a display panel to resume your original course along the former railway. Caton Low Mill is a short distance away to the right although mainly hidden by trees. After passing through two small gates, a few metres apart, re-cross the green metal bridge across the Lune to reach the car park at the Crook o' Lune.

Walk 25: Hest Bank

This provides an easy walk for anyone with a love of water. The outward leg follows the twists and turns of the Lancaster Canal while the return is along the foreshore of Morecambe Bay.

Route: Hest Bank Station – Hest Bank Marina – Lancaster Canal – Bolton Town End – Bolton-le-Sands – The Shore – Red Bank Farm – Morecambe Lodge – Hest Bank Station.

Start: Foreshore car park by Hest Bank Station. Map reference 468666.

Distance: 4 miles (6.5km)

Map: "The Forest of Bowland and Ribblesdale", number 41 in the O.S. "Outdoor Leisure" series.

Public Transport: Hest Bank is served by frequent daily buses (including Sundays) from Lancaster, Morecambe, Carnforth and Kendal. Hest Bank railway station is no longer in use.

By car: Hest Bank is on the A5105 between Morecambe and Carnforth. If travelling by the M6 Motorway leave at Junction 35 and follow the directions for Carnforth. From Carnforth head south along the A6 but fork right along the coast road in Bolton-le-Sands. Opposite the Post Office in Hest Bank turn right over the level crossing which is controlled by traffic lights. The car park is just beyond the level crossing. There is a small charge.

Tea Shop 1

Situated by the car park entrance, the Beach Cafe is all that a beach café should be but frequently isn't. Externally it is a plain, single storey rectangular building with a patio on which stand a number of tables and chairs for anyone wishing to enjoy their refreshments without leaving the sunshine or the refreshing sea breezes.

Internally it is equally simple with plain, cream walls and large windows commanding views across Morecambe Bay. The walls are decorated with photographs of steam engines, bird charts for ornithological patrons and posters showing the different breeds of dogs. The wooden tables are of modern design and there is a small shop selling plastic buckets and spades, kites, beach balls, children's fishing nets, postcards and sweets and chocolates.

There is a wide range of home-made fruit pies, gateaux, cakes and scones, all of which are served with fresh cream. There is a choice of tea, coffee or soft drinks. For something a little more sustaining the Beach Cafe offers fish and chips, beefburgers, bacon buns, beans on toast or sandwiches.

Many beach cafes disappoint but this one does not. It is scrupulously clean, the atmosphere is friendly, the service impeccable and the plain fare deliciously well cooked and temptingly presented. It makes many pretentious establishments look shabby and uninviting. To add to the interest of your visit your meal will be accompanied by the sounds of Inter-City and local trains passing behind the cafe, often at great speed.

Opening Times: Daily from Easter to the end of October, 10am to 6pm. Winter, Saturday and Sunday 10am to 4pm. **Phone:** not applicable.

Tea Shop 2

Located on Station Road, on the opposite side of the railway to the Beach Cafe, are the Victorian Tea Rooms. Small but cosy, the purple table-cloths have been carefully chosen to match the floral curtains. There is exposed stonework and wooden panelling. The wooden tables with their glass tops are surrounded by spindle-backed chairs. Again, pictures of steam engines are featured in the decorations but accompanied in this case by others of local scenes while the shelves boast a collection of decorative mugs.

Afternoon Tea is a speciality but the menu also includes scrambled eggs on toast, bacon buns, toasted teacakes, Ploughman's Lunch and salads. Not surprisingly there is a selection of scones, cakes and gateaux, all home made and served with gargantuan portions of cream.

Opening Times: Summer, Tuesday to Friday 10am to 5pm. Saturday and Sunday 10am to 6pm. Closed Mondays except Bank Holidays. November 25th to Easter, Saturdays and Sundays only, 10am to 4pm. **Phone:** not applicable.

Morecambe Bay

Morecambe Bay is a landscape of atmosphere. At full tide under blue skies with the sun reflecting off the water, it presents a vast, uplifting panorama set against the backdrop of the Lake District Fells. Under grey clouds, with the distant peaks swathed in mist and the extensive mudflats exposed, its has a sombre, threatening feel. The ten miles or so that separate Hest Bank from the Cumbrian coast around Arnside and Flookborough are extremely treacherous as many travellers in the past have found to their cost. In the days before the railway was built it was customary for stage coaches to cut across the sands of Morecambe Bay to save time on the long journey around by land. Subject to the rapidly rising tides, many never reached their destination.

This crossing of the sands has become extremely popular in recent decades with rambling clubs and other groups but this is recommended only in the company of the official guide appointed by the Duchy of Lancaster. At the time of writing this is Mr. Cedric Robinson of the Guide's Cottage in Flookborough. Through being out on the Bay every day only he is aware of the swiftly changing channels forged by the swirling waters of the rivers which enter the Bay, rivers such as the Kent, the Keer, the Duddon and the Levens.

Hest Bank foreshore is also a nature reserve managed by the Royal Society for the Protection of Birds. In winter it becomes the feeding ground for thousands of wading birds which fly in from all parts of Britain and Europe.

Under no circumstances should anyone attempt to cross the bay without the official guide. The second section of this route skirts the edge of Morecambe Bay and is perfectly safe except when there is an exceptionally high tide. In this case there is a signed alternative route using the headlands.

Lancaster Canal, Hest Bank

The Route

Leave the car park by passing to the right of the Beach Cafe and bending round to the left over the level crossing before proceeding a few extra metres to meet the A5105. Cross into Station Road, recognisable by the Hest Bank Post Office on the corner. Climb for 100 metres until reaching the Crescent.

Cross directly to a narrow opening with a Lancaster Canal sign on a gatepost. Ascend the short flight of stone steps which provides access onto the towpath by a black and white finger post showing the various distances from Hest Bank Marina.

Turn left in the direction of Tewitfield and Kendal. Pass under a small, arched stone bridge, number 118, to be met by a view of Morecambe Bay on your left and bungalows on your right. This sharp contrast continues almost without interruption until you leave the canal but most of the houses have gardens running right down to the opposite bank. Most are well-tended and in summer provide a constant succession of varying colours.

As the canal follows a snake-like course northwards there is a succession of wild flowers along the towpath including red campion, ragwort, birdsfoot trefoil, bramble and butterbur. In summer swallows dart overhead while mallard, moorhen and the occasional mute swan grace the water.

The second bow bridge is festooned with ivy and, a short distance beyond, Warton Crag and the Howgill Fells come into view. Pass, but do not use, a small footbridge with white railings. Instead pass beneath Bridge number 121, recognisable by its concrete balustrade.

Continue along the towpath looking for the milestone at Bolton Town End which reveals that you are six miles north of Lancaster and 21 from Kendal.

On approaching the next bridge, another arched affair, and opposite a large white house, turn left up a short flight of steps and pass through a squeezer stile to emerge onto a narrow road.

Turn left down the hill, passing a small memorial green on your left with several benches. A small engraved plaque, fixed to a large boulder, explains that the oak tree behind was planted in May, 1995, to commemorate 50 years of peace since the ending of the Second World War.

On reaching the A5105 cross into St Michael's Lane which now passes through some residential property before crossing the railway line to climb between hedgerows for approximately 100 metres before descending towards the sea. After passing Sandside Caravan Park the narrow road winds its way through a small collection of cottages to reach "The Shore".

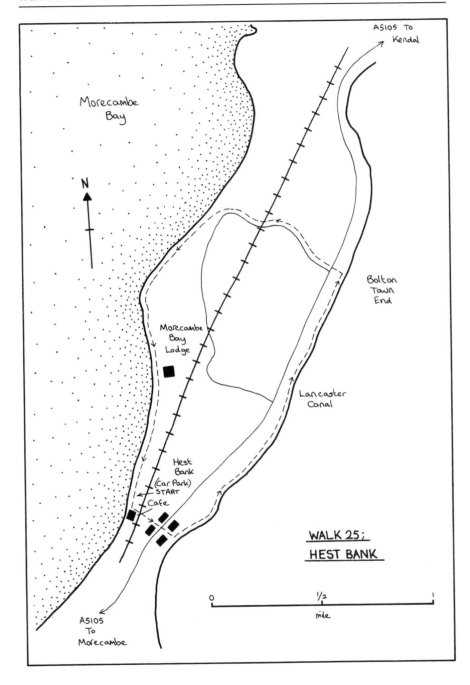

A5105 To
Kendal

Morecambe
Bay

N

Bolton
Town
End

Morecambe
Bay
Lodge

Lancaster
Canal

Hest
Bank
(Car Park)
START
Cafe

WALK 25;
HEST BANK

A5105
To
Morecambe

0   ½   1
         mile

Ignore "The Shore", which in reality is a continuation of St Michael's Lane. Instead advance to a footpath sign and there turn left along the grassy embankment which initially runs parallel to "The Shore".

From this vantage point there is a wonderful view out over the vast mudflats of Morecambe Bay with the hills of the Lake District in the background. It is a vast open-air arena which, in winter, is filled with thousands of wading birds. In summer it resounds to the song of the skylark.

At the end of the embankment veer slightly to the right towards a waymarker post on the actual shore to follow the path which forms a section of the Lancashire Coastal way, a route which links Merseyside with Cumbria.

Continue along this for more than one and a halfkm. By Morecambe Lodge cross a track edged with large boulders which leads to the water's edge. En route you pass two small headlands on your left.

Eventually, by a red brick house with a mock-Tudor upper storey, veer leftwards to another waymarker and then proceed along the raised embankment until reaching your starting point in the car park.

Walk 26: Leighton Moss

Using woodland and field paths this route takes us through delightful limestone country where, in summer, flowers are abundant.

Route: Leighton Moss – Red Bridge – Hawes Water – West Coppice – Yealand Hall Allotment – Yealand Storrs – Leighton Hall – Home Farm – Grisedale Farm – Leighton Moss.

Start: The RSPB reserve, Leighton Moss, near Silverdale. Map reference 477751.

Distance: 6 miles (9.5km)

Map: "Grange-over-Sands", number 636 in the O.S. "Pathfinder" series.

Public Transport: There are two buses hourly from Lancaster and Carnforth. On Sundays there is an hourly service. There are three buses daily from Morecambe. Silverdale station, close by the reserve, is served by several daily (including Sundays) trains from Carnforth and Barrow-in-Furness.

By car: Leave the M6 Motorway at Junction 35 and turn north along the A6. After two miles turn left to Yealand Conyers and follow the signs to Leighton Moss. There is a large car park at the reserve.

The Tea Shop

The Tea Rooms occupy a large area of the upper floor of the Visitor Centre at the Leighton Moss Reserve of the RSPB. They are housed in a converted barn which was formerly part of Myers Farm. Not surprisingly there are thick stone walls and large wooden beams.

The round wooden tables are matched by spindle-backed chairs to provide a pleasant ambience enhanced by a display on the walls of traditional farm implements such as spades, scythes, and, most unusually, an eel fork, a reminder that these creatures were once a common feature of the surrounding marshland. Not surprisingly, there are also pictures of various bird species, especially those indigenous to the area.

The Tea Rooms boast a most impressive list of speciality teas including English Breakfast, Darjeeling, Assam, Ceylon, Cinnamon, Earl Grey and fruits. There is a similar choice of coffees and soft drinks. For those cold days of winter, there is home-made soup with roll while the general menu includes Quiche Lorraine, toasted sandwiches, baked potatoes, open and closed sandwiches and salads. Home-baked scones, served with ample portions of jam and cream, are a speciality of the house. Few walkers will be able to resist sampling the freshly-cooked Apple Pie or the range of tempting gateaux and cakes which includes, amongst several others, carrot, chocolate and flapjack.

Opening Times: Daily, all year, 10am to 5pm. Closed Christmas Day.
Phone: 01524 701601

Leighton Moss

As long ago as 3,000 BC the area currently occupied by the bird reserve was a tidal inlet, its shores probably occupied by a Bronze Age settlement. In time, this inlet became blocked by silting-up which led to the formation of a sand-bar thus permitting flooding only by the high Spring Tides. This transformation encouraged vegetation to develop which, in turn, led to the creation of peat beds. During the nineteenth century drainage of the resultant marshland was attempted with the aim of converting it into valuable agricultural land. One relic of this operation are the remains of a pumping station at the chimney at nearby Crag Foot.

Because of difficulties experienced during the First World War the

Leighton Moss RSPB Reserve

attempts at drainage were abandoned in 1917 but, because of the quality of the peat extracted, the area became known as "The Golden Bowl". Afterwards the moss was flooded and in 1964 the area was leased from the Leighton Hall Estate by the RSPB. Ten years later the Society bought it outright for £64,000. Today it is renowned as one of the few breeding places in Britain for the Bittern, Bearded Tit and Marsh Harrier. There are numerous other species of both wetland and woodland birds while the reserve is noted for its colonies of breeding otters, eels and red deer.

The Route

Leave the car park by the small wooden gate close by the entrance and turn left along the road. Ignore the signed bridleway on the right after 200 metres, instead climbing slightly for a further one hundred metres to a sign on the left indicating a footpath to Red Bridge.

Turn left through the squeezer stile and continue gaining height through limestone outcrops and to the left of a patch of gorse. From the crest of the rise aim for the junction of two stone walls in the left-hand corner of the field. Negotiate the stone step stile and cross the golf course to another stone step stile some twenty metres to the left of an obvious five-barred gate.

Continue in the same direction through the trees until meeting a wide track. Turn left for a short distance. Where the track loses height slightly and bends to the right, look for a large, square flat piece of limestone by the right-hand side. Although barely recognisable because of the vegetation, there is a small abandoned quarry at this point.

At this spot turn left onto an unsigned footpath and wind your way through the trees to a stone step stile which provides access to the railway line. Exercising extreme caution because there are bends in both directions, cross directly to a flight of wooden steps over the facing wall. On the far side of this wall turn sharply to the right for a climb of some 50 metres alongside a wall on your right to reach a small wicket gate by a footpath sign.

Emerge onto a narrow, metalled lane opposite a house called "The Barn". Turn right and descend the hill to pass Red Bridge Farm. As the gradient levels continue beyond an impressive row of limestone houses on the left and several individual bungalows while approaching Hawes Water Moss on your left. Beyond "Lakeside Cottage" the lane becomes a rough track as it enters Gait Barrows National Nature Reserve which is owned and managed by English Nature.

The track, signed as a footpath to Hawes Water, passes through deciduous trees where jays screech and there is a constant flapping wings high in the canopy. On reaching a wooden barrier turn right over a stile and remain to the left of a wall as it corners after twenty metres to reach a waymarked stile.

Although the yellow arrow points forward, turn right over another, adjacent stile and cross a rough track directly to enter a field through a gateway. Keep straight ahead, immediately to the right of a stone wall until reaching a tall ladder stile on your left. Do not negotiate this. Rather, turn right along a clear path which ascends a gentle slope and passes through a gap in a derelict wall before reaching a squeezer stile adjacent to a wooden five-barred gate on the boundary of the Gait Barrows Nature Reserve.

Beyond, follow the grassy lane with a wall on your right and a deciduous wood on your left. On reaching a T-Junction at the top of the slope turn right through a wooden five-barred gate onto a narrow path which quickly develops into a green, grassy swathe as it levels and takes a clear course through a mixture of bracken and hawthorn.

After almost a kilometre it meets a wide, sandy track on a bend. Maintain your general direction along this new track to Yealand Hall Allotments where the villagers once enjoyed grazing rights. Lose altitude to a five-barred gate and stay with the lane for a considerable distance until reaching a green, metal five-barred gate by a footpath sign.

Through the gate is a road junction. Turn left to follow the road signed to Yealand Redmayne, Carnforth and Milnthorpe. After 100 metres and on the first bend, look for a footpath sign to Leighton Hall by the far corner of "The Old Smithy". Turn right through a wicket gate and, with "The Old Smithy" on your right, negotiate a metal five-barred gate after five metres and bend to the right with the obvious wide track. This stays to the left of a wall and, subsequently, of a hedge.

Beyond the next five-barred gate the field path transfers to the right of the hedge and passes through several more gates until emerging onto a wide surfaced track by a footpath sign. Leighton Hall Home Farm is but a short distance to your left. (For a visit to Leighton Hall turn left).

Turn right along this track to reach Grisedale Farm after half a kilometre. Pass the farm buildings and proceed until meeting a Y-junction alongside a stone barn. Fork right. After 200 metres a five-barred gate allows access to Leighton Moss Reserve. The unsurfaced bridleway is flanked on both sides by head-high reeds which restrict any views. Along the way it is possible to enter the public hide for a view across the mossland and to observe any birds which may be present.

After more than a kilometre the bridleway reaches the road. Turn left for the final 200 metres to the main entrance to the reserve and that welcome Afternoon Tea.

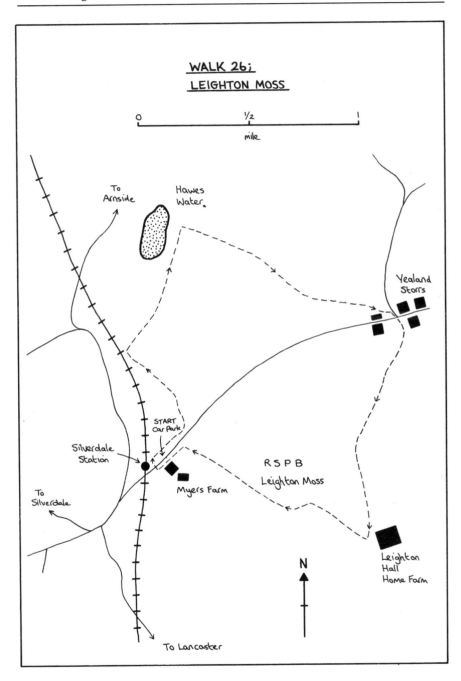

WALK 26;
LEIGHTON MOSS

0   ½   1
              mile

To Arnside

Hawes Water.

Yealand Storrs

START Car Park

Silverdale Station

To Silverdale

Myers Farm

R S P B
Leighton Moss

Leighton Hall Home Farm

N

To Lancaster

Walk 27: Waterslack

A short, gentle route along field paths and bridleways through Gait Barrows National Nature Reserve and around the shores of Hawes Water.

Route: Challan Hall – Red Bridge – Hawes Water – Challan Hall.

Start: Challan Hall, Silverdale. Map reference 475766.

Distance: 2 miles (3km)

Map: "Grange-over-Sands", number 636 in the O.S. "Pathfinder" series.

Public Transport: Two buses hourly from Lancaster and Carnforth from Monday to Saturday. Hourly on Sundays. Three buses daily from Morecambe. Trains from Carnforth and Barrow-in-Furness daily to Silverdale including Sundays. Silverdale station is approximately one kilometre from the start which is served by the "Silverdale Shuttle", a local bus service which connects with trains at Silverdale Station from Monday to Fridays.

By car: Leave the M6 Motorway at Junction 35 and turn north along the A6. After threekm miles turn left for Yealand Conyers (signed) and follow the signs for the RSPB Reserve at Leighton Moss. At the junction a few metres beyond the reserve, turn right, pass the railway station and Challan Hall is a short distance beyond on the right. There are several spots for off-road parking.

The Tea Shop

The Tea Rooms at the Waterslack Garden Centre are housed in a wooden pavilion. The walls are lined with pine tongue and groove and the wooden tables are partnered by wooden spindle-backed chairs. For those fine, sunny days there are tables outside.

On offer are soups and light lunches, sandwiches and "Waterslack Treats" which include Quiche Lorraine, Ploughman's Lunch, "Waterslack Delight", a mixture of prawns, salmon and tuna With Yoghurt Herb Sauce and Steak Toast. There are scones with whipped cream and pancakes with jam or maple syrup. The extensive selection of home-made cakes includes shortbread, chocolate cake, lemon cake and carrot cake.

Opening Times: Summer 9.30am to 5pm. Winter 9.30am to 5pm. Closed Mondays and Tuesdays. **Phone:** 01524 701862.

Hawes Water

The Route

Take the track to the right of Challan Hall, which is signed to Silverdale, for a distance of 50 metres to reach a stile. Nearby is a display panel informing us that we are about to enter the Gait Barrows National Nature Reserve which is owned and managed by English Nature.

Over the stile aim for the waymarked post before proceeding down the mole-infested slope to a fence corner on the left by two redundant gateposts and some hawthorns. Stay to the left of both gateposts and then walk to the right of a fence. Where this corners away to the left continue forward under overhead wires to a facing stile.

Exercising caution, cross the railway line to a white ladder stile and then remain to the left of a stone wall to a footpath sign and another stile which provides an exit onto a road.

Turn left for a short distance and then left again into an surfaced lane soon losing height rapidly to pass Red Bridge Farm on your right. As the going levels continue beyond an impressive row of stone-built limestone houses on your left and several individual bungalows.

The lane loses its surface as it enters the Hawes Water National Nature Reserve owned by English Nature and becomes signed as a footpath. On reaching a wooden barrier turn right over a stile and then remain to the left of a wall as it corners to the left after twenty metres to reach a waymarked stile. Turn left over this and then right, as directed by the waymark. The clear path initially passes between two fences some ten metres apart and then through the trees.

After crossing a culverted stream, the fence is on the left only. To your right are several limestone outcrops. Eventually the path bends round to the left to reach a waymarked T-junction. Continue round to the left as the path develops into a bridleway pursuing its level course through the mixed deciduous trees for several hundred metres.

Then it embarks on a gentle climb to the right of an ivy-covered stone wall to pass through a wooden five-barred gate to meet the road a few metres to the right of Challan Hall.

To visit the Waterslack Tea Rooms, turn left and walk for approximately 400 metres.

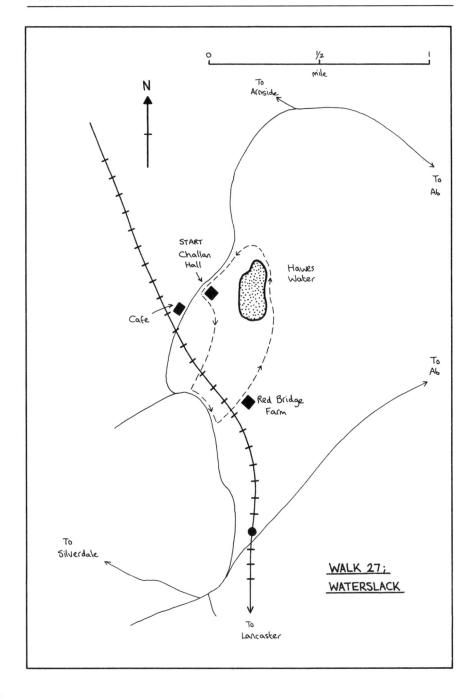

WALK 27;
WATERSLACK

Walk 28: Silverdale

A walk along the coast followed by a climb over the summit of
Warton Crag before returning to Silverdale.

Route: Silverdale – Lindeth Tower – Jack Scout's Wood – Jenny Brown's Point
– Quakers' Stang – Crag Foot – Warton Crag – The Beacon – Crag
Foot – Fleagarth Wood – Silverdale.

Start: Wolf House Galley, Silverdale. Map reference 463742.

Distance: 8 miles (13km)

Map: "Grange-over-Sands", number 636 in the O.S. "Pathfinder" series.

Public Transport: Silverdale is served by two buses hourly from Lancaster and Carnforth
from Monday to Saturday all year. Hourly service on Sundays. Three
buses daily from Morecambe. Trains from Carnforth and
Barrow-in-Furness daily, including Sundays. There is a local bus
service from Monday to Friday, "The Silverdale Shuttle", which serves
the local area and connects with trains at Silverdale Station.

By car: Leave the M6 Motorway at junction 35 and turn north along the A6.
After two miles turn left to Yealand Conyers and follow the signs to
Silverdale. The Wolf House Gallery is at the southern end of the
village, from where it is signed. It is close to Gibraltar Farm. There is
limited off-road parking by the Gallery.

The Tea Shop

The Tea Room at the Wolf House Gallery is housed in the former
shippon of a farm, still retaining the stalls and buskins from its previous
existence. These are matched by the flooring of stone flags and quarry
tiles and the ancient wooden beams, unchanged since the building was
erected about 1700, or perhaps even earlier.

The name of the gallery is derived from the coat-of-arms which is still
to be seen above the studded door of the farm house: "Homo Homini
Lupus", which translates as "Man is a Wolf to Man". Wolf House Gallery
and Tea Room command extensive views of Morecambe Bay, especially
out over the estuary of the River Kent.

The menu is restricted to beverages and cakes but suffice it to say
that one cake will inevitably lead to another. All are baked on the

premises by joint owner, Denise Dowbiggin, using only fresh ingredients including eggs from their own Silky Hens.

The range includes scones, served with conserves and cream, Flapjacks, Millionaire's Shortbread, Chocolate Cake, Lemon Cake and many others. These may be accompanied by any one of a number of speciality teas or their own house blend of freshly-ground coffee. For those hot, lazy days of high summer there is also a selection of fruit drinks or milk.

One word of caution. Keep an eye open for Toby, the pussy with an addiction for scones. Let your attention wander for a second and he will have yours off your plate and inside his tummy.

Opening Times: 1st April to 24th December, Daily 10.30am to 1pm and 2pm to 5.30pm. Closed Mondays. January to March inclusive, Saturdays and Sundays only, 10.30am to 5.30pm. **Phone:** 01524 701405.

Silverdale

Silverdale forms part of the Arnside and Silverdale Area of Outstanding Natural Beauty. It is noted for its well-defined and thinly-wooded limestone hills, some of which afford extensive views over the surrounding countryside and out over the estuaries of the Rivers Kent and Keer.

In the past the village was noted for its fishing, mainly cockles and mussels, and for its pastoral farming. Today there are only two working farms in Silverdale. The fishing, mainly restricted to neighbouring Flookborough, was unique in that it used neither boats nor baits. Highly dependent on the fisherman's knowledge of the local weather and tides, the cockles were found about a centimetre below the sand and were raised to the surface by the use of "Jumbo Boards". These consisted of a flat piece of wood with two handles and were employed for beating the surface. Once they had risen, the cockles were collected and stored in large bags which were subsequently carried to the shore by horse-drawn carts. Today the horses have been replaced by tractors.

There is considerable evidence that the area was settled by Neolithic Man followed by Bronze Age Man. In more recent times the area was occupied by Norsemen sailing across from their settlements in Ireland. The name "Silverdale" is believed to be derived from that of a Norseman, "Selredal", "The Owner of the Dale.". During the nineteenth century Silverdale started to develop industrially with the production of lime for the emerging steel industry of Furness and also became known for its copper smelting, the mineral being mined near Jenny Brown's Point. This led to the construction of a quay for the export of the finished products. Sometimes, dependent on the shifting sands and the state of the tide, portions of this quay may still be seen.

Copper smelting chimney, Jenny Brown's Point

Later in the same century the village grew as a resort but expansion in this direction was restricted by the mercurial nature of the sands and beaches and the presence of so many rocky outcrops.

The Route

From the parking area outside the Wolf House Gallery walk for some twenty metres to the road junction and turn left, following the narrow, surfaced road signed to Jenny Brown's Point, soon passing both Gibraltar Farm and Lindeth Tower on your right.

Gibraltar Farm, one of the two which remains working in Silverdale, was probably so-named following Sir George Rooke's capture of Gibraltar from the Spaniards in 1704. Lindeth Tower is associated with Mrs. Gaskell, who frequently stayed there while planning and writing some of her novels.

Continue for several hundred metres until reaching a gate on your right bearing a National Trust sign indicating Jack Scout Wood. This area, now a pleasant area of greensward dotted with hawthorn and gorse, was once renowned for its industrial activity, particularly for the burning of limestone. It was bought by the National Trust in 1982 and shortly afterwards the lime-kiln just beyond the gate was restored.

Turn right through this gate and then turn left to pass just to the right of the restored kiln. Continue along the distinct path as it follows a course roughly parallel with the road towards the sea. In summer this area is a haven for lime-loving plants and the butterflies they attract.

After several hundred metres the path reaches a kissing gate on the left which provides access back onto the road a short distance before some enormous rocks protrude into the sea.

Through the kissing gate turn right to cross a cattle grid with a disused quarry on your left to reach Jenny Brown's Point.

From here there are sweeping views out across Morecambe Bay which include Heysham Nuclear Power Station, Arnside and the Bowland Fells. Thoughtfully, the Parish Council has provided a seat where people can relax while enjoying the fine prospect.

Proceed along the narrow road as it rounds Jenny Brown's Point to reach a five-barred gate immediately in front of Brown's Houses. Fork right onto the clear footpath along the foreshore as directed by a large white arrow.

Brown's Houses, a single building containing several cottages, may originally have been associated with Dikes Farm, the name "Dike" being given to the channels by which the water escapes across the sands when the tide is out. The farm was probably one of the first in the district to be built of stone. The name of Brown was associated with that of a man who either held land or farmed in this area in the sixteenth century. The name "Jenny" may have been that of either his wife or daughter.

The path passes to the right of Brown's Houses before leading to a limestone chimney which is well preserved following restoration. This was not constructed in association with lime burning but is a remnant of the copper smelting industry which took place here late in the eighteenth century.

From the chimney the path maintains direction across the grassy foreshore, the turf being of such excellence that it would be a credit to Old Trafford. Eventually, having passed an isolated and redundant stile, it reaches a waymarked one some twenty metres beyond. Continue forward along the same line for a further 250 metres to a 4-armed finger post at the foot of Heald Brow.

Turn right and, keeping a fence on your left, follow the embankment path across the estuary which is signed to Fell Foot and forms part of the Lancashire Coastal Way. After approximately one kilometre turn left over a stile to walk between two wire fences, approximately 25 metres apart, until reaching another stile. Over this stay forwards towards a facing metal five-barred gate. However, do not use this.

Instead turn right through another five-barred gate which is waymarked and cross a substantial stone bridge over a drainage channel.

At the far end of the bridge you meet a track and a 2-fingered footpath sign. Turn left along the track, pass under a low railway bridge and continue to the road.

Turn right along the road towards Crag Foot. After a short distance, and by the telephone kiosk at the road junction, turn left into the driveway leading to Moss House Farm. There is another limestone chimney on your right.

A short distance before reaching the farmhouse, turn right into a walled lane but, after thirty metres, turn left as directed by a white sign, to pass through a gap in the fence before embarking on a gradual climb through birch woodland. As the track traverses pastures turn left through a gate before swinging right through yet another gate.

At the subsequent Y-junction fork left and continue until reaching a stile bearing a yellow waymark.

Over this turn sharply to the right, staying to the left of a wall and to the right of a green bin suspended from a tree until meeting a white footpath sign nailed to another tree. Advance up the slope through a landscape reminiscent of the Cotswolds to reach a squeezer stile in the facing drystone wall. Beyond, continue forward for ten metres to a track. Turn left and stay with this track until it emerges onto the Coach Road.

Turn right along the Coach Road in the direction of the village of Warton which has very close associations with the family of George Washington, the first President of the United States, and which flies the Stars and Stripes from the church tower on the 4th July every year.

However, Warton is not on our route. After several hundred metres and just before the first houses of the village, turn right into a bridleway signed to Crag Foot. Within the first hundred metres you pass the entrance to Warton Crag Nature Reserve.

As the lane climbs the views over the Howgill fells, Pine Lake and the Lune Valley open up to reveal the flat summit of Ingleborough in the very far distance.

After emerging from the woodlands the route levels into a walled lane. By the first 3-armed finger post turn left along the narrower path which climbs somewhat more gradually for approximately one kilometre to the Triangulation Pillar at 163 metres above sea level. Almost alongside is The Beacon, a metal brazier atop a thick pole which marks the site of the original beacon which was ignited in 1588 to announce the approach of the Spanish Armada. Also nearby is the site of an Iron-Age Fort.

From the Beacon retrace your steps for 100 metres and, by another

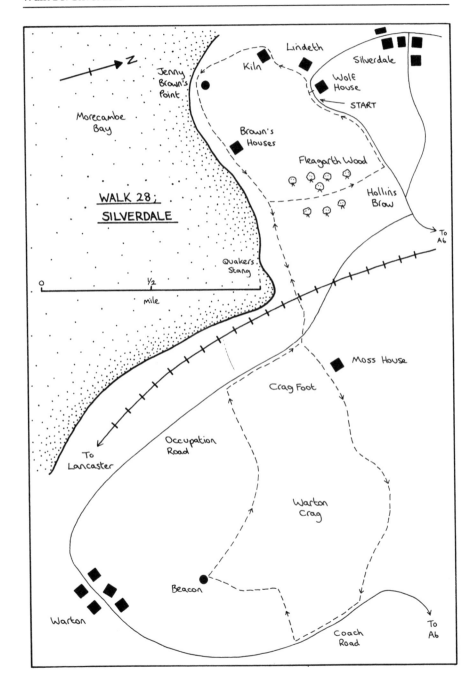

finger post, veer leftwards for a gentle descent along a grassy path running by several limestone outcrops. After passing through a five-barred gate turn left to re-join the original bridleway for the rapid descent towards Crag Foot.

On gaining Occupation Road turn right, losing even more height until joining your outward route near the telephone kiosk and the entrance to Moss House Farm.

Retrace your steps across the embankment until reaching the 4-armed finger post at the foot of Heald Brow. Turn right along the path signed to Hollins Brow. Initially this has a fence on the right and shortly begins to climb before curving round towards the left to reach a stone step stile marking the entrance to Fleagarth Woods.

The path, now widened into a track, continues climbing for a considerable distance before levelling to meet Hollins Lane by a footpath sign. Turn left along Hollins Lane, now surfaced, and continue by the former hospital on the left and Hazlewood Farm on your right until reaching the Wolf House Gallery where you can enjoy your refreshments and look around the crafts.

Walk 29: Lancaster

A tour of this ancient city with its historic buildings and narrow alleyways.

Route: Tourist Information Centre – Judges' Lodgings – Maritime Museum – Trinity Church – Castle – Market – Sun Street – Assembly Rooms – Dalton Square – St Leonardsgate – Church Street – Tourist Information Centre.

Start: Tourist Information Centre, Lancaster, map reference 475517

Distance: 2 miles (3km).

Map: 1. "The Forest of Bowland and Ribblesdale", number 41 in the O.S. "Outdoor Leisure" series. 2. Town plan supplied by the Tourist Information Centre.

Public Transport: Rail: Lancaster is on the main West Coast Route between London and Glasgow. Frequent daily trains from London, Birmingham, Manchester, Manchester Airport, Liverpool, Glasgow, Edinburgh, Preston, Barrow-in-Furness and Crewe. There is a frequent daily service to Leeds via Skipton. There are also frequent daily bus services to Lancaster from London, Manchester, Glasgow, Edinburgh, Aberdeen, Barrow-in-Furness, Skipton, Morecambe, Kirkby Lonsdale, Kendal, Keswick and other principal cities.

By car: Lancaster in on the A6. It may be reached from the M6 Motorway by leaving at Junction 33 for Lancaster South or Junction 34 for Lancaster North. From Skipton and other parts of Yorkshire it may be reached by using the A683 from Kirkby Lonsdale.

The Tea Shops

There is an abundance of tea shops and cafes in Lancaster city centre. Two have been selected, both being on the route of this walk.

Tea Shop 1: O'Malley's

This is located in Bashful Alley, one of several ancient narrow thoroughfares in the centre of Lancaster. Appropriately, the tea room has a Dickensian atmosphere with its wooden floors, old beams and bow windows with small panes set into thick stone walls. The polished dark wooden-topped tables are partnered by spindle-backed chairs while one side is divided into cosy cubicles by the use of pew-like benches.

Specialities of the house include All-day Breakfast, Lamb Hot-Pot, Meat n' Tattie Pie and similar dishes. Specials, listed on the blackboard, are changed daily. Karen Morris and her staff are very proud of their home-baked cakes ranging from Millionaires' Shortbread to Smudgy Chocolate Cake and including Walnut Cake, Full o' Fruit Pie, Passion Cake and Muddy Cake. Scones smothered with jam and cream are always available. There is a wide choice of both teas and coffees.

Opening Times: All year, Mondays to Saturdays 8.30am to 5pm. Closed Sundays. **Phone:** 01524 36561.

Tea Shop 2: Sunbury Coffee House

Located in Music Room Square this is the epitome of Georgian elegance with its classical proportions, decorative friezes and plaster mouldings. This atmosphere is enhanced by the marble-topped tables supported by single cast-iron legs, spindle-backed chairs and thick carpets.

It specialises in offering a bewildering range of coffees from Kenyan to Blue Mountain and including, amongst many others, Lancaster Blend Peaberry. This is matched by an equally impressive choice of speciality teas.

The Sunbury is also noted for both its Afternoon and Cream Teas with delicate sandwiches followed by scones dripping with preserves and cream and a choice of home-made gateaux. These are too numerous to single out. For a rather more substantial repast, if that were possible, the Sunbury offers filled baguettes, croissants and sandwiches, both open and closed.

Opening Times: All year, Monday to Saturday, 8am to 4pm. Closed Sundays. **Phone:** 01524 843317.

Lancaster

Despite its long and distinguished history the city of Lancaster has only recently started to capitalise on its attractions. It has been overshadowed as a tourist centre by its close neighbour, Morecambe, and has also suffered from being positioned between the Lake District and the Yorkshire Dales. It was the place that people passed by. However, during the last few years the City Council has developed a more positive approach to marketing its many historical attractions.

The city occupies a strategic crossing of the River Lune, a factor first appreciated by the Romans who built a fort on the same site now occupied by the Castle. The only major relic of this period to have survived is the Roman Bath House which was discovered and excavated in 1973 and 1974.

The chief glory of Lancaster is the Castle which was founded shortly after the Norman Conquest of 1066, although the impressive Gatehouse is the work of Henry IV, Duke of Lancaster, and still belongs to the Queen in her role as Duke of Lancaster.

Close by is the Priory Church occupying the site of the first monastery recorded in the county. Founded in 1094, it is still principally medieval in character and one of its glories is the King's Own Regiment Memorial Chapel.

During the medieval period Lancaster commenced its development as a port and by the eighteenth century was one of the major ports of the country with a flourishing trade with America and the West Indies, dealing especially in cotton, coffee and tobacco. During this period many warehouses were built along St George's Quay. They still stand, having been converted into flats.

Not surprisingly there developed a flourishing social life centred around the Assembly Rooms, the Music Room and the Grand Theatre. Some outstanding town houses were built.

During the nineteenth century, however, the port declined, principally because of the silting-up of the River Lune and the construction of larger ocean-going vessels. In an effort to maintain its position the town tried to develop Sunderland Point and, when this failed, looked for an alternative at Glasson Dock. Neither flourished although Glasson remains a working port, principally for coastal vessels.

The nineteenth century saw Lancaster become one of the major producers of linoleum and furniture, thanks to the enterprise of the Williamson and Gillow families. Its importance as a centre of communications was further enhanced with the building of the turnpike roads and, a short while afterwards, of the Lancaster Canal. Disappointingly, this never became a part of the national network and its importance remained local. Not so the railway which linked the city with London and Glasgow directly. Today it is one of the most important stations on the West Coast main line with branches to Skipton, Leeds and Barrow-in-Furness. In the 1960s Lancaster was selected as one of the sites for a new university.

The Castle

Occupying the site of a former Roman fort, the Castle was commenced shortly after the Norman Conquest by Roger of Poitou. The dominating

The Judges' Lodgings, Lancaster

Great Keep, increased in height at the time of the Armada scare, originally dates from about 1200 and dominates not only the rest of the site but the city itself. Part of the Castle remains in use as a prison but certain areas, notably the eighteenth century Shire Hall, Hadrian's Tower, the Crown Court, the cells and the Drop Room, where prisoners were prepared for the gallows, are all open to the public. The magnificent Gateway may have been built by King John.

Opening Times: Easter to October, 10am to 5pm. Guided tours only. There may be times when these hours are changed. Check with the Tourist Information Centre.

The Priory Church

This was originally a part of the Benedictine Priory which was founded in 1094 and closed in 1414. Most of the present church dates from the fourteenth and fifteenth centuries. It is noted for its splendid choir stalls, Anglo-Saxon cross fragments and the Memorial Chapel of the King's Own regiment.

Opening Times: Easter to October, daily 9.30am to 5.00pm.

The Maritime Museum

This is housed in the former Custom House on St George's Quay which was designed by Richard Gillow in 1764. With its classical facade and stone pillars it is one of the glories of Lancaster. Its exhibits tell the story of Lancaster's history as a port and there are sections devoted to the Lancaster Canal, the River Lune and the Morecambe Bay gas field.

Opening Times: Easter to October, daily including Sundays, 11.00am to 5.00pm. November to Easter, Daily including Sundays, 2.00pm to 5.00pm.

The Judges' Lodgings

Reputedly the oldest town house in Lancaster, this was originally owned by Richard Covell, the notorious witch baiter. Later it provided accommodation for the judges visiting Lancaster for the Assize Courts. Today it houses an exhibition of Gillow's furniture and the Museum of Childhood.

Opening Times: These vary. Phone 01524 32808 for details.

The City Museum

This is to be found in the former Town Hall which was built between 1781 and 1783. The ground floor is occupied by changing exhibitions while the upstairs is devoted to the history and archaeology of Lancashire.

Opening Times: All year, Monday to Saturday, 10am to 5pm. Closed Sundays.

Dalton Square

This was created by the Dalton Family from nearby Thurnham Hall on the site of a former Dominican Friary. It was designed as a high class residential area but was never fully developed because of the decline of Lancaster as a port. It is dominated by the Town Hall and an enormous statue of Queen Victoria which was donated to the town by Lord Ashton whose wealth was based on the linoleum trade.

The Route

Leaving the Tourist Information Centre, itself occupying a former warehouse, turn right and, after only a few metres and by the Cottage Museum, bear right down the hill to the Covell Cross behind which stands the Judges' Lodgings.

At the junction with China Street make another left turn so proceeding down the hill with a car park on your left. At the foot of the hill turn left again onto St George's Quay with the River Lune soon appearing on your right.

The left-hand side of the Quay is lined with former warehouses, many now converted into flats. Continue as far as the Maritime Museum with its splendid classical facade.

After visiting the Museum turn right along the Quay but take the first turning on your right so that you walk to the left of the Museum. By the far corner of the building turn left and proceed behind the former warehouses for 15 metres before veering right onto the path which climbs through Vicarage Fields.

At the first T-junction make a right turn to reach a footpath sign after 20 metres. Turn right up a flight of steps to another footpath sign after 100 metres. By this turn left to follow the distinct path over the field to the Roman Bath House.

Retrace your steps to the footpath sign and there turn left to climb the hill while enjoying the view over Morecambe Bay and towards the Howgill Fells and Ingleborough.

At the top of the hill ascend the steps to enter the churchyard of the Priory Church with the replica Armada Beacon on your right. Continue forwards to another footpath sign and turn left in the direction of the Shopping Centre. Pass between the Priory Church on your left and the Castle on your right with a view of the folly in Williamson Park directly ahead in the distance.

Proceed down the steps alongside the Castle and, by the far corner and by St Mary's Gate, turn right into St Mary's Parade and then back into Castle Hill. At the junction by the Post Office make a right turn into Meeting House Lane to visit the Friends' Meeting House.

Retrace your steps as far as the Post Office and then continue a short distance to China Street. Cross directly into Market Street. After 20 metres turn right into Bashful Alley for a visit to O'Malley's Tea Rooms.

Return to Market Street and turn right. After a further 20 metres turn left into Sun Street to reach Church Street and the Music Room, passing Sunbury's Coffee Lounge on the way. Turn right along Church Street but, after 20 metres and by the Royal Bank of Scotland, turn right into New Street to pass Lancaster Public Library on your left.

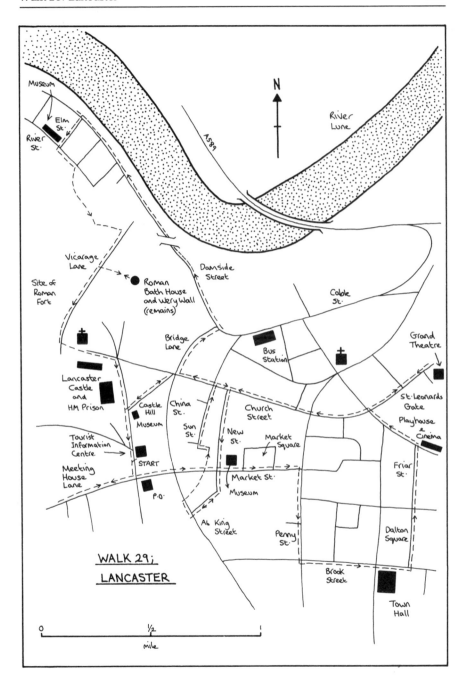

WALK 29;
LANCASTER

Continue as far as Market Square and the former Town Hall which is now the City Museum. Proceed along Sir Simon's Arcade, another narrow alleyway and, by the new market, turn right for a distance of some 20 metres to emerge onto King Street, opposite the Assembly Rooms, now housing a craft shop.

Retrace your steps to Market Street and turn right to pass "The Blue Anchor" pub on your left. This has recently been the subject of excavation which revealed the existence of a medieval thoroughfare which has now been incorporated into the building by Mitchell's, the Lancaster brewery.

On reaching the junction opposite St Nicholas's Arcades, a modern shopping complex, turn right into Penny Street and continue as far as its junction with Common Garden Street. There turn left and proceed forward into Brock Street as far as Dalton Square, the Town Hall and the statue of Queen Victoria.

Stay to the right of the statue and, by the far corner of the Town Hall, make another left turn to walk along the far side of Dalton Square before entering Friar Street. Continue to the far end where the Duke's Theatre stands.

Turn left into Moor Lane where, at the nearby junction, is a fountain erected to the memory of a local solicitor, Thomas Johnson, who devoted so much of his energy to working on behalf of the local youth.

By this fountain turn right and proceed along St Leonardsgate as far as the Grand Theatre, one of the oldest in England and restored for the production of plays and concerts by local groups.

Retrace your steps to the junction with Moor Lane, then continuing forward across Rosemary Lane to re-enter Church Street. Walk to the far end by the Covell Cross before retracing your steps up Castle Hill to the Tourist Information Centre.

Tea Shop Walks – Spreading everywhere!

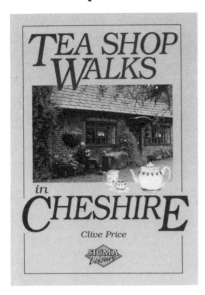

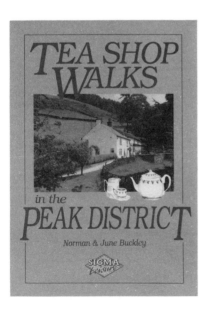

The Sigma Leisure Tea Shop Walks series already includes:

Cheshire

The Chilterns

The Cotswolds

The Lake District, Volume 1

The Lake District, Volume 2

Leicestershire & Rutland

North Devon

The Peak District

Shropshire

Snowdonia

South Devon

Staffordshire

Surrey & Sussex

Warwickshire

Worcestershire

The Yorkshire Dales

Each book costs £6.95 and contains an average of 25 excellent walks: far better value than any competitor!

WALKS IN MYSTERIOUS LANCASHIRE
Delving into a host of mysterious places throughout Lancashire, Graham Dugdale's collection of 30 walks appeals to walkers with enquiring minds. Lucid walking directions and the author's ornate, hand-drawn maps complement the entertaining commentary. £6.95

TOWNS & VILLAGES OF BRITAIN: LANCASHIRE
Full of historical facts and liberally laced with tales of hauntings, witchery and enchantment - the moors, valleys and mossland of Lancashire are the backdrop to Michael Smout's comprehensive gazeteer of the county's towns and villages. "The histories of our towns and villages neatly gathered in one definitive guide" – SOUTHPORT VISITER £8.95

BEST PUB WALKS IN LANCASHIRE
Lancashire has a rich pub heritage and a surprising variety of countryside. This book, by Neil Coates, is the most comprehensive guidebook of its type. £6.95

WEST LANCASHIRE WALKS
No need to venture into touristy areas, it's all on the doorstep for Lancashire's walkers - "Knowledgeable guide to 25 rambles by the Ramblers' West Lancs Group Chairman" RAMBLING TODAY. £6.95

EAST LANCASHIRE WALKS
This companion volume to "West Lancashire Walks" leads you to an abundance of walking and places of interest which lie just beyond your urban doorstep to the East - a haunted house near Warrington, an American Wood at Aspel, there's even a giant on the banks of the Mersey! £6.95

50 CLASSIC WALKS IN LANCASHIRE
Terry Marsh again shares his vast experience to explore the good walking country and places of beauty within the county's boundaries - known to the locals but waiting to be discovered by the wider population. £7.95

In case of difficulty, or for a free catalogue, please contact:
SIGMA LEISURE, 1 SOUTH OAK LANE, WILMSLOW, CHESHIRE SK9 6AR.
Phone: 01625-531035; Fax: 01625-536800.
E-mail: info@sigmapress.co.uk   Web site: http//www.sigmapress.co.uk

VISA and MASTERCARD orders welcome.

 **MAGAZINE**

 **EVENTS**

 **COMPETITIONS**

 **MEMBER DISCOUNTS**

 **TASTINGS & SAMPLING**

 **A FREE GIFT WHEN YOU JOIN**

Tea is our most social and sociable drink – a part of our national heritage and daily life for well over 300 years. The Tea Club exists so its members can share and enjoy the history, traditions and romance associated with this fascinating drink.

THERE'S SO MUCH MORE

TO TEA THAN JUST

A CUPPA !

HOW TO JOIN

Simply send your name, full address and postcode to:

The Tea Club

PO Box 221

Guildford, Surrey GU1 3YT

and an application form will be sent to you immediately.

Tea Club Memberships are also a great gift idea – why not send one to a friend !